TEACHERS MATTER

TEACHERS MATTER

The Trouble with Leaving Political Education to the Coaches

Stephen M. Caliendo

PRAEGER

Westport, Connecticut
London

Library of Congress Cataloging-in-Publication Data

Caliendo, Stephen M., 1971–
    Teachers matter : the trouble with leaving political education to the coaches / Stephen M. Caliendo.
        p.   cm.
    Includes bibliographical references and index.
    ISBN 0–275–96907–X (alk. paper)
    1. Political science—Study and teaching (Secondary)—United States.   2. United States—Politics and government—Study and teaching (Secondary)   3. Political socialization—United States.   4. United States. Supreme Court—Public opinion.   5. Public opinion—United States.   I. Title.
    JA88.U6 C24   2000
    320′.071′273—dc21   99–086109

British Library Cataloguing in Publication Data is available.

Library of Congress Catalog Card Number: 99–086109
ISBN: 0–275–96907–X

First published in 2000

Praeger Publishers, 88 Post Road West, Westport, CT 06881
An imprint of Greenwood Publishing Group, Inc.
www.praeger.com

Printed in the United States of America

The paper used in this book complies with the Permanent Paper Standard issued by the National Information Standards Organization (Z39.48–1984).

10 9 8 7 6 5 4 3 2 1

For Patricia and Amelia

Contents

Contents

Tables and Figures

TABLES

FIGURES

Preface

This book is the result of two simultaneous interests in which I have been engaged over the past ten years: a desire to understand the base of the Supreme Court's legitimacy as it functions as a counter-majoritarian institution; and a regard for the role of formal political education in perpetuating legitimacy for the existing political system. The former was inspired by an interest in constitutional law, while the latter derived from my struggle to boost my own teaching through reflection and study of pedagogy and curriculum theory. At some point (though I cannot exactly determine when) I realized that the two were related—that our socialization ensured that we would have a great deal of support for even the most undemocratic (in the colloquial sense of the word) institution. As I continued to consider how powerful the implicit messages in my own teaching could be, I began to think about my colleagues at both the secondary and post-secondary levels who have not been as reflective. Intentional perpetuation of some unstated norm is one thing, but how much have we "taught" our students that will ultimately be more powerful than any overt political messages that may leak into our lectures and class discussions?

In the political communication literature, there is a consideration of the difference in media effects from so-called straight news stories as opposed to editorials. The argument is that when we read an editorial (or hear or see one), our defenses are up, as we recognize the information as "biased," but when we read straight news, we expect that we are getting objective truth. Consequently, when bias is present in straight news (as it invariably must be), it is more likely to affect our attitudes than the blatant messages in an editorial. A parallel can be made with social studies education: those teachers who insist on spouting dogma around the classroom (from both sides—we have all been in their classes) may actually be less likely to affect students' attitudes as those who attempt to be "neutral" or "objective," since students will not have cause to question whether the information is "true."

This situation is exacerbated by the tendency to give exams and quizzes that ask students to recall and recite information, rather than think critically about that information. One trend that I noticed in my research is that teachers almost always refer to the course textbook as "the book," and not by the author's name. This suggests that there is no perspective in the book—indeed, it is *the* book, perhaps dropped down from the Government gods, containing all the important truths that one must learn to pass the course and become a good citizen. Not unlike the effect of a straight news story, the students and teachers do not challenge the information contained in the readings because the authors do not present the information as anything but absolute facts. Controversies between policies may be revealed, but never are the students asked to think (as they say in corporate America) "outside the box." That box, in this case, is the American constitutional system. Any dilemmas that face the American polity, we learn, exist within that box, and therefore need to be solved within that box. There may be nothing wrong with the box. The box may be great. But students should be encouraged to understand that it exists and that its sides are cardboard, not steel. In a democracy, the people make the box, and the people can change the box. The sides of the box are stiffened by the way we educate our children about their place within it. It was my intention to find out exactly how (and maybe even why) this was happening. The following pages document that work and are at once troubling and encouraging. Teachers do, indeed, matter, and we need to make sure that they are equipped with the tools to facilitate a truly democratic educational experience for our children.

There have been an amazing number of people who have made this project possible for me. I greatly appreciate the level of cooperation and patience from all of the teachers, administrators, and students who were involved in the spring of 1997. Many of the ideas herein have come from lengthy (and often late-night) conversations with my dear friend, Stephen Medvic. He along with so many of my other personal/professional friends—Amy Zeitler, John McGeady, David Jones, Barbara Palmer, Rich Pacelle, and Fenton Martin—helped to make this possible with unending support and encouragement. Bill Kyle, Sil Lenart, Bill Shaffer, Eric Waltenburg, and Rosie Clawson were extremely helpful to me with regard to this project and, more important, my broader professional development. I would not have reached this point without them. Most prominently, my friend and mentor, Mark Gibney has been instrumental to my development as a teacher, a researcher, and a person. While repayment is impossible, my appreciation for his time and energy (especially on the tennis court) is eternal.

Finally and most importantly, I need to recognize my family. I am indebted to my ancestors who brought their families to this country in order to give my generation a chance; to my parents and brother for pushing me through the hard times, particularly when I was younger; and to my wife, Patricia, for being as understanding as humanly possible over the past seven years. She has been my most reliable base of support, as well as my most honest critic. This book would never have been finished if it were not for her love and patience.

Chapter 1

Introduction

It is not uncommon in the United States to turn on talk radio or read a letter to the editor in a local paper wherein a concerned citizen laments low voter turnout or perceived public apathy by noting that "people in other countries are killing each other for rights we take for granted!" Consistently low levels of traditional forms of participation and a decline in what some scholars have termed "social capital" suggest that America's schools have been less than effective in educating America's youth for citizenship. This book takes a hard look at the way American students are being educated to participate in their political world.

The title of this book may seem obvious to many. Of course teachers matter! But in what ways do they matter? Political scientists have believed for some time now that teachers do not really matter all that much. Studies in the late 1960s and early 1970s suggested that attitudes formed during early political socialization were not as rigid as once believed since attitudes were found to change over time. This is not surprising due to the politically turbulent nature of the times under consideration and the burgeoning media. In other words, whereas agents of socialization like the family and the schools were found to be quite good predictors of adult attitudes in the first half of the twentieth century, the times (with apologies to Bob Dylan) were a-changin'. American culture was becoming increasingly information-saturated. And if that was the case then, it is clearly that much more the case today. Many of the political attitudes we form early on are likely to be challenged at some point in our lives. Others, however, will not be. It is the latter with which this study is concerned.

Further, it is those less salient attitudes that are most crucial to the legitimization of our governmental system. There is a level of acceptance of many aspects of our system that Americans fail to consider, let alone challenge. The righteousness of the Constitution is the most important example. Any discussion of public interest invariably takes place within the confines of what the Constitution has loosely prescribed. Without making any normative evaluation of that fact, it is important to acknowledge it, if for no other reason than to recognize the implicit agreement to which the vast majority of us stipulate. But there is nothing innate about that belief in the Constitution. Rather, we are taught it from a very early age. No matter how many cable channels or Internet sites appear, the mainstream political discourse will always be conducted within that unstated parameter. Understanding this changes the way we view politics and our place in the democracy. It is important, then, to examine the ways in which latent attitudes about the American political system are learned.

WHO IS TO BLAME?

So what is wrong with the citizenship education programs in American schools? Naturally, we are looking for someone (or something) to blame. It would be wonderful if we could simply point the finger at the person or institution that is messing things up, and then fix it. The solution is not that simple. It is not all the teachers' fault, and it is not all the fault of school administrators. Some of the blame resides in the universities that educate social studies teachers, but our national and social priorities are equally problematic. One might infer from the subtitle of the book that the main trouble is that so many coaches teach social science courses, but there is nothing inherent about coaching that makes a person unable to help students learn about government or any other subject in a meaningful way. The coaching problem is one of priorities.

An important part of the political socialization process in this country occurs in the schools. The schools are constantly under fire for their perceived failure to "properly educate" children (whatever that means). One of my arguments in this book is that if there are "problems" with regard to citizenship education (teaching students how to be participants in the public sphere), it stems from our lack of attention to the social sciences—to questionable priorities. When the Russians launched Sputnik in the 1950s, the United States had a supposed renewed investment in education. We know, of course, that the investment was largely in the natural sciences, so that our youth would be competitive with the technological advancements of our foes. Even though that intensity has waned, the so-called hard sciences are still privileged over the social sciences in the minds of most Americans. Psychologists are not *real* doctors; political scientists are not *really* scientists; and so on. That ranking of priorities may be having an important effect on how students (and ultimately adults) think about the most fundamental aspects of American politics.

It is not coincidental that social studies teachers just happen to be talented coaches. Rather, when looking for a place to put good coaches, the assumption seems to be that while anyone can teach Government (or History or Sociology), not everyone can teach Biology or Calculus. When the phys-ed, health and wood shop positions are filled, the social sciences are next in line. As a matter of practicality and utility, it would be difficult to argue that Trigonometry is more *important* than Government, but this is where the irony lies. Since politics is so ubiquitous (and accessible through mainstream media), we all have at least some familiarity with it, which is not the case with the natural sciences. Most of us probably feel that we could fill in as an emergency substitute in a Government class for a day or so, but we would probably be less comfortable doing so in an Algebra class. So we leave those classes to the "experts," or at least the more specifically trained. But, at the risk of offending those who teach these subjects, it is safe to say that most students' lives will be much richer if they have a meaningful understanding of government and politics, as they would be having a firm grasp of the Pythagorean theorem. Even if we subscribe to the argument that both are equally important, we need to question, then, why individuals whose priorities are other than academic are more often assigned to social sciences than natural sciences.

Again, while civic education (broadly defined) is important, I am less concerned with how many students can name their state senators and members of Congress as I am with latent attitudes related to legitimacy and system support. Accordingly, I have spent a great deal of time observing high school Government courses and talking to teachers and students about the way we learn about the most mysterious institution in our government—the United States Supreme Court.

While the Supreme Court has enjoyed greater levels of confidence among the mass public than either Congress or the presidency, researchers have been unable to explain from where this support comes. I argue that adolescent political education is a particularly important predictor of political attitudes that are out of the mainstream of political discourse (such as latent support for political institutions, especially an institution as invisible as the Court).

THE QUESTION OF PERSISTENCE

An important point about the relevance of social science education, especially with regard to Government, is that since politics is all around us, what we learn in school is likely to be challenged and subsequently changed as one moves through life anyway. While that is probably true for salient issues and concepts (like feelings about abortion, for instance), it is less convincing for attitudes that are not so obvious (like diffuse support for the structure of the system or for governmental institutions). In other words, we have to be thinking about something in order to change our minds about it. There are some topics that we think about in school but do not think about very much ever again. I have not thought about the coefficient of friction, for instance, very often since my high school Physics class. Very little harm or benefit will come by my failing to consider such a concept, but the government stands to gain (or lose) a great deal by students not considering, for example, that the two-party system may be a less-than-ideal way to elect public officials in a democratic nation. What matters, then, is the way in which we are taught about these important latent concepts relating to American politics and government because those lessons affect attitudes that are more likely to persist into adulthood.

LATENT POLITICAL ATTITUDES: SUPPORT FOR THE SUPREME COURT

The latent construct examined in this study is diffuse support for the Supreme Court. I chose to consider these attitudes for two related reasons. First, the Court is at once the least visible and the least "democratic" (in the colloquial sense of the word) national institution, and as such it provides a convenient platform from which to examine latent political attitudes at the time we pay the most attention to it: during high school Government class. Second, the Court's unique position in the political system makes it wholly reliant on other officials and agencies to enforce its decisions. Since it is the "weakest" branch in terms of not having a public mandate (since its members are not popularly elected), it benefits immensely from a socialization system that tacitly renders it above "politics as usual" and portrays it as a defender of the Constitution. Both of these reasons make the Court an excellent example for why we should reconsider formal political education as an area of research.

Since members of the Supreme Court are in this unique position of having to rely on compliance to their rulings while not being directly accountable to the people for their actions, the general acceptability and feelings of legitimacy and confidence in that institution should be of particular interest.[1] Understanding the base of the Court's support is worthy of our attention, for "if an institution loses its support . . . its activities and successes become more difficult and costly to achieve" (Handberg 1984, 4). As Lawrence Baum (1976) notes, the Supreme Court rarely makes a final decision on a case. After a decision is handed down, it is the responsibility of either a lower court or an executive agency to interpret the ruling and act accordingly. This creates a potential problem of compliance, as both courts and administrative agencies may circumvent, ignore, or simply defy higher court rulings.[2] It is unusual for the Court to make law that is in direct opposition to public sentiment (Marshall 1989), but justices must be certain that there will be compliance even to decisions that cut against the popular position of the mass public.

But issues of compliance go beyond opposition or inertia of government institutions; they extend to the response of the public as well. Interest in public support for the Court stems from the inherent importance of such support to the Court's legitimacy. Possessing "neither the purse, nor the sword," the Court is entirely reliant on voluntary compliance to its rulings by lower courts, Congress and state legislatures, and executive agencies. Throughout American history, it is easy to recall a select number of incidents of noncompliance by those lower political entities, even if such cases are few in the grand scheme of the Court's decision-making past. For example, in the 1950s, many southern states adamantly opposed the Court's decision to integrate public schools (*Brown* v. *Topeka Board of Education* 1954). This resistance was fueled by questions of the Court's legitimacy in telling people where to send their children to school.[3] More recently, prochoice groups have threatened to disregard the Court's decision if it should overturn *Roe* v. *Wade* (1973). In the face of such opposition, the Court's image is pivotal. As Richard Davis (1992) notes: "The Court's continued success in gaining compliance with its decisions is contingent on the public perception that the Court is largely apolitical" (179). In other words, if the public would begin to perceive the Court as just another political branch of government (as "legal realists" argue), there is reason to believe that groups, individuals, or even states would again disobey a ruling that they thought was contrary to their best interests.[4]

Justice Antonin Scalia, in his concurring opinion in *Webster* v. *Reproductive Health Services* (1989), reflects on threats to the Court's legitimacy when an unpopular ruling is handed down:

Alone sufficient to justify a broad holding is the fact that our retaining control, through Roe, of what I believe to be, and many of our citizens recognize to be, a political issue, continuously distorts the public perception of the role of this Court. We can now look forward to at least another Term with carts full of mail from the public, and streets full of demonstrators, urging us—their unelected and life-tenured judges who have been awarded those extraordinary, undemocratic characteristics precisely in order that we might follow the law despite the popular will—to follow the popular will (535).

If there was any doubt that the justices are not only aware of, but concerned about, public opinion, the above comments should alleviate the uncertainty. One can almost detect a hint of paranoia, or at least defensiveness, on Justice Scalia's part when he admits that the Court's powers are "undemocratic." He seems to be a bit uneasy about the possibilities of losing public support.

He is not alone. Justices Sandra Day O'Connor, Anthony Kennedy, and David Souter, announcing the opinion of the Court in *Planned Parenthood of Southeastern Pennsylvania* v. *Casey* (1992) directly address the Court's legitimacy, its base, and the possibility of its erosion:

[T]his Court cannot and should not assume any exemption when duty requires it to decide a case in conformance with the Constitution. . . . [N]o Court that broke its faith with the people could sensibly expect credit for principle in the decision by which it did that.

It is true that diminished legitimacy may be restored, but only slowly. Unlike the political branches, a Court thus weakened could not seek to regain its position with a new mandate from the voters, and even if the Court could somehow go to the polls, the loss of its principled character could not be retrieved by the casting of so many votes. Like the character of an individual, the legitimacy of the Court must be earned over time. . . . If the Court's legitimacy should be undermined, then, so would the country be in its very ability to see itself through its constitutional ideals. The Court's concern with legitimacy is not for the sake of the Court but for the sake of the Nation to which it is responsible (709).

But the Court must be concerned about its legitimacy for its own sake as well. Aside from its uniqueness with regard to enforcement, it is a government institution in a democratic setting. This alone makes it vulnerable to the will of the people.[5]

Political scientists have been struggling to explain with empirical research the reasons why the Court consistently enjoys more positive evaluations than the other two branches of the federal government.[6] Two broad lines of analysis emerge from the published research on public opinion and the Supreme Court. On the one hand, a substantial body of work has examined whether the Court's decisions are affected by public opinion (Marshall 1987, 1989; Mishler and Sheehan 1993). This research is rooted in a behavioral model of judicial decisionmaking and seeks to determine how closely the Court's decisions have followed (or at least coincided with) public opinion on salient issues. Such work relates to research on support for the Court insofar as it speaks to the amount of attention justices may or may not pay to public opinion, and subsequently implies a level of (assumed) support from the public.

Other research has focused more directly on support for the Court. The tradition with which I am currently concerned centers around survey research—whether respondents are asked about specific Court decisions, or more general feelings or attitudes toward the Court. Much of this research has addressed the concept known as "diffuse support," the working definition of which comes from David Easton. It is "a reservoir of favorable attitudes or good will that helps members to accept or tolerate outputs to which they are opposed or the effects to which they see as damaging to their wants" (Easton 1965, 273). This is contrasted with "specific support," which is support for the *actions* or *policy outputs* of an institution. Early on, research showed that specific support for Court decisions had an impact on the level of diffuse support respondents had for the Court (Murphy and Tanenhaus 1968), but more recent research has shown that not to be the case among the mass public (Caldeira and Gibson 1992).[7]

If diffuse support is pure, it must exist separately from specific support. While this continues to be a point of contention among researchers (see Segal 1995, for example), it is agreed that diffuse support comes about largely through the political socialization process.[8] This study sets out to explore the most probable root of the Court's privileged status in American politics: formal political education.

STRUCTURE AND BASIS FOR THIS STUDY

In the spring of 1997, I observed 190 high school seniors in 10 different American Government classes in a midwestern state. The data are composed of students who had 5 different teachers in 4 different schools (3 public, 1 private). Table 1.1 illustrates the composition of the classes.[9]

THIS STUDY: DATA COLLECTION

The data for this study come from three sources: teacher interviews and classroom observations, textbooks, and surveys of student political attitudes. I began to make initial contacts with school officials and teachers in the spring of 1996.[10] In the summer of 1996, I narrowed the study to five schools and began directly corresponding with school officials about the possibility of visiting and observing. I spent the fall months working out details of the project with principals, teachers, superintendents, and, in one case, the school board.[11]

There were specific details, of course, that needed to be worked out with each school. One principal, for instance, insisted that the student surveys not be given in class, but rather be sent home with the students, completed at home, and returned to me later. Another school district (with two high schools planned for the study), asked me to meet with their assistant superintendent, which I gladly did. After pitching the project to him, he agreed to consider it and bring it before the school board, where the final decision would have to be made. Further, I was to come to the school board meeting, explain the project, and answer any questions board members had about it. I agreed, and in December of 1996, I met with the school board and was subsequently notified that they approved of the study.

I issued a consent form (in duplicate) to all participants, asking that both the students and their parents sign and return one of the slips to me (not to the teacher) before any observations began. The consent form was sent home with the students along with a letter explaining the research, and providing information so that the parents could contact me with any questions or concerns. In no instance did a parent return the form with a negative response, nor did any student ever indicate to me that their parents did not want them to participate, but some students forgot to give the form to their parents and, thus, could not participate in the project.[12]

I contacted the state Department of Government at the end of May 1996 to obtain statistics as to the Government textbooks being used in the state. I received the statistics (see Table 1.2), and an Official Textbook Adoption List for the current years. I learned that four books (three publishers) comprised 95 per cent of the total adoptions and decided to focus my analysis on those texts.

CHAPTER LAYOUT

Put simply, my argument is that researchers have been unable to pinpoint the reasons for the Court's high level of confidence among Americans because they have underplayed the importance of political education for some types of political attitudes. Explaining support for the Court is an important and worthwhile endeavor, as it is a crucial aspect of American democracy. More fundamental,

Table 1.1
Composition of American Government Classes in the Study

School	Teacher	Class	N	% female	% nonwhite	% rural	% college bound	% at least one parent w/college education
School 1	Mr. Kaupas	1	9	62.5	11.1	85.7	100.0	44.4
		2	21	81.0	5.0	75.0	95.2	23.8
		3	14	50.0	0.0	84.6	78.6	35.7
School 2	Mr. Caballero (Catholic)	1	23	52.2	4.3	30.4	95.7	73.9
		2	23	30.4	17.4	9.1	91.3	91.3
School 3	Mr. Hawk	1	20	70.0	5.0	50.0	90.0	70.0
		2	15	30.8	7.1	50.0	85.7	46.7
School 4	Mr. Peralta	1	15	60.0	0.0	46.7	85.7	40.0
		2	24	62.5	8.3	58.3	95.8	62.5
	Mr. McGill	1	26	48.0	12.0	70.8	76.0	42.3
TOTAL			190	54.8	7.5	52.7	89.2	55.3

Note: Schools 3 and 4 are in the same school district. Only students who participated in the survey of political attitudes are included.

Table 1.2
Textbooks Adopted for American Government in Target State (1991-1997)

Publisher/ Book(s)	Percentage of Districts Adopting
Glencoe	23%
American Government: Principles and Practice by Mary Jane Turner, Kenneth Switzer, and Charlotte Redden	
United States Government: Democracy in Action by Richard C. Remy	
Houghton Mifflin	20%
Government in America by Richard J. Hardy	
Prentice Hall	52%
Magruder's American Government by William A. McClenaghan	
Others	5%

however, is understanding the way our children are being educated with regard to politics.

Chapter 2 contains a brief description of the theory underlying this study. In chapter 3, I examine adult attitudes toward the Supreme Court over the past twenty-five years, controlling for several of the variables that have been found to influence support for the Court in various cross-sectional studies. In chapter 4, the teachers explain their perceptions of the responsibility they have for educating citizens for democratic participation. Differences between the teachers will become apparent. Since the high school Government class is generally structured around the textbook, popular Government texts are analyzed in chapter 5. Results of the student surveys and a model of student support for the Court appear in chapter 6, while chapter 7 contains a discussion of the state of political education in America, as well as suggestions for ways to improve the system.

NOTES

1. Indeed, researchers have been interested in this question for years. In his seminal piece on decisionmaking and democracy, Dahl argued that the Supreme Court was not,

for any length of time, a staunch defender of minority rights. He warned that the Court jeopardizes its legitimacy "if it flagrantly opposes the major policies of the dominant alliance" (1957, 293). Dahl was measuring public opinion as manifested in the elected officials of Congress and the White House. Johnathan Casper later challenged Dahl's findings on the bases that (1) he neglected to consider several aspects of the Court's activities (such as its role in statutory construction), and (2) the Warren and Burger Courts were consistently active in protecting minority rights (1976).

2. See Giles, Cataldo, and Gatlin (1976); Dometrius and Sigelman (1988); Hansen (1980); and Johnson (1979).

3. See Berkman and Kitch (1986).

4. To advance its apolitical image, the Supreme Court has chosen to conduct most of its business in secrecy and surround itself with mystery so as not to challenge its symbolic place in American democracy (see Davis 1994).

5. See Mondak and Smithey (1997) for a mathematical model that estimates erosion and subsequent return of support for the Supreme Court.

6. Tom Tyler (1990) even goes so far as to say that "the concept of 'legitimacy' has been taken for granted [and] . . . empirical evidence is scarce" (27).

7. Jennifer Segal (1995) found that agreement and disagreement with the Court's policy decisions is significantly related to diffuse support. Similarly, C. Scott Peters (1995) reports that specific support and diffuse support are related. Segal and Peters both used undergraduate students to conduct controlled experiments, thus, their findings may not be contradictory to those of Caldeira and Gibson (1992) since those authors found a relationship to be present among opinion leaders. Since college students are generally more educated and come from more financially secure backgrounds than the average citizen, Segal and Peters may have been measuring attitudes of "opinion leaders."

8. Indeed, the above excerpt from *Planned Parenthood* v. *Casey* (1992) reminds us that "the legitimacy of the Court must be earned over time." The justices are as much aware of this as political scientists are.

9. A small number of students who were enrolled in the classes were omitted from the study because they failed to return permission slips that were required if they were to participate.

10. I was able to test the survey instrument in the fall of 1995. Using a pilot sample of college students in introductory political science classes that semester, I was able to see what questions were good, what things I still needed to ask, and if the order of the questions affected responses. I used two forms of the survey and distributed them randomly. One form had questions designed to measure attitudes about specific Court outputs (abortion, capital punishment, and prayer in school) *before* questions about diffuse support for the Court, while the other form had the order reversed. There were no statistically significant differences in the way students with the first form answered either set of questions as compared to those who had the second form. Therefore, the order of these items generated no threatening "cueing" effect.

11. It was at this point that one school was eliminated from the study. After several letters and telephone calls that largely went unanswered, I took a trip to the school one afternoon to meet with the assistant principal. I learned that, based on previous experiences, the school was concerned about how parents would react to their children partaking in a survey. After convincing the assistant principal that none of the questions was sensitive in nature, he promised to take it to an administrative meeting. I was notified shortly thereafter that the administrators agreed to allow me to conduct my project, pending approval by the teachers who would be involved. It was this stipulation that

would threaten, and eventually kill, the project at this large school. It turned out that only two of the three Government teachers would be teaching Government in the spring, and neither of them wanted an outsider coming into their classes. While this loss was a serious blow to the number of students I would eventually be able to survey, it did not affect the variation with regard to socioeconomic status (the other schools would certainly suffice in that regard). I suspect, however, that it did reduce variance with regard to race and urban/rural residence.

12. The students were more conscientious than I had anticipated, and I received approximately 200 forms back of the 256 I distributed (78 per cent).

Chapter 2

Political Socialization and Political Education

Unless a society is able to fashion some bond between a member and its political authorities, regime, and political community, no kind of political system could possibly endure.

—David Easton and J. Dennis (1969, 68)

Political socialization is more important in explaining latent attitudes in adulthood (such as diffuse support for the Supreme Court) than attitudes toward more salient political institutions, actors, and issues. The reason is quite simple: adults will constantly have their attitudes about many aspects of political life challenged or reinforced throughout life as more and more information concerning those things comes forth. Such is the nature of political socialization. According to Dean Jaros, "early socialization may be displaced or overridden [sic] by later socialization, nullified by adult experiences or even by deliberate countersocialization" (1973, 57).

We receive political information primarily through the media and through interpersonal communication. The two are, however, related; people do not generally discuss political issues that either do not affect them personally or are not covered in the news.[1] The U.S. Supreme Court is covered less frequently than the other branches of government in the media and is thus unlikely to be considered by most Americans on a regular basis. Therefore, the attitudes about the Court that were developed when people *did* think about that institution are more likely to persist into adulthood than other political attitudes.

THE SUPREME COURT AND THE MEDIA

Richard Davis (1994) has done some of the most comprehensive work on media attention to the Supreme Court. In the preface to *Decisions and Images: The Supreme Court and the Press*, Davis discusses how precious little work has been done in this area and explains that this may be a result of the common "assumption [that] the Supreme Court has no constituency similar to those of the members of Congress or the president. The Court's constituency, it is argued, is the legal profession" (xii). But as Davis notes, this assumption is unfounded. Since the Court has no power without public support, it is necessary to examine what kind of information about the Court reaches the American public. Like most political information, the mainstream media is almost solely responsible for providing that information during adulthood.

There is considerably more media attention paid to the Court today than there was even fifty years ago. David O'Brien (1993) reports that

[i]n the 1930's, less than half a dozen reporters covered the Court on a regular basis. . . . By the late 1950's, there were full-time reporters from the United Press International (UPI), the Associated Press (AP), a few major newspapers, and a couple of more specialized legal periodicals, such as *U.S. Law Week*. In the last three decades, the number of reporters steadily increased to about thirty, with a core group of regular journalists about half that number. All three major television networks, along with Cable News Network, have regular reporters at the Court (353).

Despite this increase in coverage, however, the American public is not exactly inundated with stories about the Court. Doris Graber (1997) reports that over a one-year period (August 1994 to July 1995), the three major networks devoted a combined hour and a half to the Court, while the president and Congress received over fifty-two hours and eleven hours, respectively (271). Elliot Slotnick and Jennifer Segal's (1998) study of television news during the 1989 and 1994 Court terms also reveals that there are not many stories about the Court at all, and those that do appear are often short (thirty seconds or less) and only reported by the news anchor, as opposed to more in-depth coverage by a correspondent (187). These researchers conclude that there is a "difficulty of being apprised of the Court's activities through watching the news" (24). In the ever-increasingly visual world of multimedia and cable, this finding is particularly striking. In the words of Slotnick and Segal (1992), "[i]t is difficult to view our data without being struck by the relative paucity of Court coverage for much of the news year" (24). Indeed, it is this lack of information about the Court from the media, year in and year out, that suggests a prominent role for political socialization in the formulation of attitudes about the Court.

Davis (1994) argues that the Court deliberately manipulates the press for both the preservation of institutional power and the implementation of policy preferences (xii). By allowing itself to be perceived as unanimous, independent, distant from other political institutions and public opinion, and immune to political pressure, the Court has been able to maintain its legitimacy in the eyes of the American public (4-8). Part of this manipulation comes by way of the se-crecy with which the Court chooses to surround itself. By not delivering press conferences, conducting the decisionmaking in private, and not allowing cam-eras in the courtroom, the Court has maintained a cloak of mystery within which it operates year in and year out.

Aided by the Court's Public Information Office (PIO), the press only receives information that the Court deems necessary: "By screening press requests, of-fering the official information the Court provides, facilitating press access to the aspects of the Court's activity that the justices want known, and aiding in closing off access to other facets of the Court, the public information officer helps communicate the messages designed to foster the desired image of the Court" (Davis 1994, 53). This information is not generally very notable. Most of what comes from the office is trivial information about the justices in order to provide color for filler in stories (Davis 1994, 50). Such activity is illustra-tive of the difference between the public image construction of the Court and that of the other branches of government. Since the other branches' members are constantly in the public view, the job of their public relations offices is gen-erally to "spin," or redirect emphasis about the members' actions. For the Court, however, the decisions are expected to speak for themselves, and any-thing behind or beyond those decisions is generally kept out of the press.

Consistent with the notion that justices benefit by remaining relatively anonymous to the mass public, Court stories do not involve discussion (or even mention) of individual justices. Davis (1994) reports that an average of 9.8 per cent of CBS News stories about Court cases from 1984 to 1989 mentioned a justice's name.[2] *Time* magazine was considerably higher with an average of 37.3 per cent of case-related stories mentioning a justice during that same pe-riod.[3] The Associated Press—from which many local papers and stations get their stories about national news—mentioned an individual justice in just 15.9 per cent of their case-related stories. While it is not surprising that *Time* maga-zine was most likely to feature the name of a justice in its stories, what is nota-ble about these data is that newspapers and broadcast news very rarely report anything about justices individually when they report on Supreme Court cases. If a justice joins the majority, writes a concurring opinion, or fails to ask ques-tions during oral arguments, he or she is not likely to be mentioned in the news story about the case. Justices are mentioned when they write an opinion on a salient case or argue a particularly notable dissent, but even in these instances, the justices, "unlike presidents, cabinet members, or congressional leaders, . . . return to obscurity during most of the rest of the year" (135).

Davis's contrast of the justices' image with that of other elected and appointed officials (the "political" public servants) is at the heart of the issue at hand. It is precisely because of the justices' obscurity—which contributes to the institu-tion's mystery—that early attitude formation is particularly relevant with regard to the Court.

THEORETICAL AND EMPIRICAL FACETS OF POLITICAL SOCIALIZATION

Political socialization research emerged in the 1950s and tapered off considerably by the late 1970s. Interest in the subject was sparked by the trend toward research on the behavioral aspects of the political world, and away from institutional, legalistic approaches to studying politics. Spawned from psychological theories of cognition and development, political scientists began to apply that field's knowledge and techniques to the study of political learning—a study particularly important in democratic societies. For instance, Orit Ichilov (1990) notes that "[t]he unique characteristics of democracy and democratic citizenship . . . must . . . be given careful consideration. From both philosophical and practical vantage points, the viability of democracy greatly depends on the voluntary acceptance of the democratic way of life by citizens" (1).[4]

M. Kent Jennings and Richard Niemi (1974) reflect that agents of socialization are generally divided into three or four main categories, in order of importance: family and school, peer groups, and a loosely labeled "other agents" class, which includes "the mass media, secondary groups, political events, as well as idiosyncratic factors that affect groups or individuals" (24-25).[5]

Early Studies

Herbert Hyman's groundbreaking review of political socialization research, *Political Socialization: A Study in the Psychology of Political Behavior* (1959), served to further interest in what quickly became a recognized subfield of political science. In his summary of the literature, Hyman discusses the "great" influence of one's family on political orientation and party identification (71) and notes that "other agencies of socialization" (age group, peers, school, college education) may be responsible for a child's departure from his or her parents' political attitudes (71-96). And so began a tradition of social science research aimed at explaining the transmission of political attitudes to the young.

Because parents seemed to be the primary source of political learning, work in the 1960s tended to focus on preadolescent children. The prevailing notion was that whatever political and social attitudes were to pass from parent to child, they would do so early on in the child's cognitive development. Fred Greenstein explains that "during the last five years of elementary school, children move from near—but not complete—ignorance of adult politics to awareness of most of the conspicuous features of the adult political arena. And the fourth and eighth graders live in quite different psychological worlds" (1965, 1). Combining case studies and questionnaire responses of some 650 children in New Haven, Connecticut, Greenstein (1965) examined children's attitudes on political authority, knowledge of political information, and degree of partisanship, suggesting differences with regard to socioeconomic background and gender. Further, he found that affective attitudes precede cognition; that is, children indicate a party preference before they understand the differences between the parties or can even name an elected official from their professed party. These affectively attained attitudes were normatively positive toward support for authority figures and the existing political system. This "benevolent leader" theory, as it came to be known, dominated socialization research in its early iterations (Greenstein 1960; 1965). Greenstein found that "political socialization seems to be conservative in its effects. Socialization processes foster the status quo through the perpetuation of class and sex differences in political participation, continuity between the generations in party preferences, continuation (and perhaps even strengthening) of adult assessments of the relative importance of political institutions" (1965, 158).[6] The Court is able to maintain high levels of confidence because its image (and that of its members) and legitimacy go relatively unchallenged in the daily lives of Americans—particularly when compared to the president and members of Congress. But in order for the Court to ensure compliance to its decisions, it need not maintain a high level of popularity with regard to its day-to-day decisionmaking. Again, the Court will be able to sustain even widespread disagreement with particular rulings, however salient they may be, if it can maintain a level of diffuse support, as described by Easton (1965).

Theoretical Development

Easton's (1965) systems-analysis approach to studying politics suggests the role of political socialization, but the theory was more clearly articulated a few years later (Easton and Dennis 1969). Here, the authors advocate a "political theory of political socialization," by which they mean a theory with an "objective . . . to demonstrate the *relevance* of socializing phenomena for the operations of political systems" (18, emphasis in original). They endorse the development of a higher theoretical framework within which empirical research on political socialization can be placed. This might be contrasted with earlier studies that take concepts derived from the adult world, "such as party identification, political interest, political information, and issue orientations or ideology," and merely try to explain them based on childhood learning patterns (Easton and Dennis 1969, 20-21). With regard to Easton's systems-theory approach, the authors ultimately ask how political socialization may contribute to or detract from the persistence of a given political system, even under stresses (50-51).[7]

Empirical Studies

The nadir of empirical political socialization research occurred during the 1970s. Unlike the earlier empirical works (Greenstein 1960, 1965; Connell 1971; Andrain 1971), the focus shifted from preadolescent learning to a more comprehensive behavioral approach to the acquisition and development of political attitudes.[8]

The most notable of these works is Jennings and Niemi's (1981) longitudinal panel study of parents and their children in 1965, followed up in 1973. This is the most comprehensive and ambitious empirical project dealing with political socialization, as it was able to examine both generational and age changes, along with period effects that might impact shifts in political attitudes. What they found challenged commonly held beliefs of the time:

For a time, some researchers were convinced that development of political attitudes crystallized prior to late adolescence. When that position became untenable it became fashionable to believe that development and change continued through early adulthood. While precise limits were rarely asserted, it seemed to be commonly assumed that rigidity had set in at least by age 30. We are now taking issue with even that limitation on adult changeability. Without denying that young adults change more frequently than older persons, and that the likelihood of change is less as one gets older, we argue that older adults are far from intractable (387).

When adult attitudes change, it is in response to changes in their personal and social environment (389). Still, Jennings and Niemi's data support the notion that change in political attitudes is less likely as one ages. The significance of this finding, however, is to suggest that attitudes formed during the early and adolescent socialization periods are not as rigid as once believed.[9]

But adult attitudes about less salient issues are unlikely to change for two related reasons. First, since age acts as a barrier (however permeable) to change, some notable shift in the political environment would be necessary. In this case, such a shift would have to involve the Court. Second, such low levels of information about the Court reach most adults that challenges to their earlier beliefs, as noted above, are rare.

Having established that adult attitudes change primarily when there is some challenge to them, and that the mainstream media provide little in the way of information that could potentially challenge attitudes about the Supreme Court, I now move to a discussion of the primary period when Americans develop attitudes—attitudes that are likely to persist—about the Court: time spent in school.

POLITICAL EDUCATION

While families and schools are considered to be the primary agents of socialization, family matters more indirectly with regard to attitudes about the Court than does the school system. Lack of media coverage provides less of an opportunity for children to pick up information and attitudes about the Court from their parents; if there is nothing newsworthy to discuss, it generally will not be discussed. What children can learn about the Court at home, however, may be a function of broader attitudes about the American justice system. As the highest court in the land, such attitudes are likely to surface when a survey respondent is asked to think about the relatively invisible and mysterious Supreme Court.[10] Any direct information about the Court, however, will be learned in school—more specifically, in the high school civics or American Government course. What is the role of these courses in the American political system? Do they merely provide support for the existing political regime, or do they provide an opportunity for students to question and ponder political issues beyond the parameters of the existing system?

The Role of the Schools

Educational and political thinkers acknowledge that citizenship education is more than teaching the structure and procedure of American government. Rather, "it consists of a set of complex formal and informal educational processes that attempt to instill appropriate knowledge, skills, values, and behaviors in youth who are destined to become citizens of the American republic" (Dynneson and Gross 1991, 5). But there is continued discussion among educators and educational theorists as to the "proper" role of schools in the democratic process.[11] The United States Department of Education endorses an approach compatible with the functional needs of a democratic society: "It has been recognized since the founding of the nation that education has a civic mission: to prepare informed, rational, humane, and participating citizens committed to the principles of American constitutional democracy" (Center for Civic Education 1994, v). This is consistent with Greenstein's contention that political socialization largely reinforces the status quo. Effectively, standards such as these, laid out by both federal and state governments, are tools in the self-perpetuating cycle of American constitutional and political norms.[12]

Regardless of normative perspectives on citizenship education in general, the high school social studies curriculum plays a unique role by providing students information about their social and political worlds. The process of socialization is complicated and is by no means confined to the schools. Pamela Johnson Conover (1991) explains that after nearly a half decade of interdisciplinary research, the term "political socialization" has become convoluted. It really consists of four parts:

- *political learning* is "the learning of any politically relevant material regardless of whether or not this learning promotes support for the existing regime, and likewise regardless of whether or not the learning is deliberate" (131).
- *political socialization* is "narrower than political learning[;] it only includes learning that generally promotes support for the existing regime" (131).
- *political education* is "the deliberate effort to transmit political information or to create affective political orientations . . . [w]hether or not such learning supports the political regime" (132).
- *civic education* refers to "the deliberate teaching of attitudes and values that are compatible with support for the existing regime" (132).

Figure 2.1 represents graphically the relationship among these concepts. I am primarily concerned with political education, since I make no *a priori* assumption about the intention of the school system to perpetuate the Court's legitimacy.[13]

Early in the study of political learning, Kenneth Langton and Jennings (1968) concluded that the civics curriculum in American high schools is not "even a minor source of political socialization" (388). Consistent with earlier findings of University of Michigan researchers (especially Campbell *et al.*, 1960), Langton and Jennings imply that differences in political knowledge and attitudes are largely a function of other agents of socialization—presumably the family above all else.

Figure 2.1
Types of Political Learning

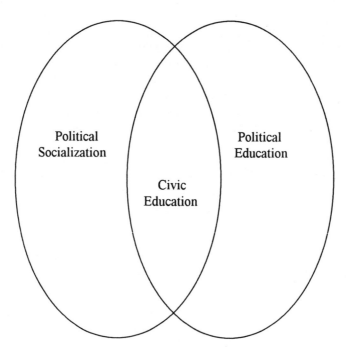

Political Learning

Political attitudes that are more salient are most likely to change since they are constantly being challenged by new information and perspectives. Figure 2.2 depicts a continuum upon which three levels of latency are placed. Political orientations, once argued to be the most latent of political attitudes, are actually more salient today than ever before. Unlike specific attitudes about political issues, these middle-level constructs are likely to be transferred from one's parents. But, as Jennings and Niemi (1974) found, even these can be altered as a person matures. In a media-dominated culture that is swimming with terms like "liberal," "conservative," "moderate," "Republican," and "Democrat," Americans encounter these concepts and ideas on a daily basis.

The high school curriculum is more likely to have an effect on concepts that are less salient than party identification or political participation, and it is likely to play a large role in the formation of attitudes concerning confidence in political institutions—especially about the least salient institution in American political culture.

Figure 2.2
Levels of Latency of Political Attitudes

Least Latent (most open to change)

policy preferences

ex: spending on foreign aid
budget considerations

political orientations

ex: partisanship
racial attitudes

support for political institutions

ex: level of confidence or trust
commitment to the system

Most Latent (least likely to change)

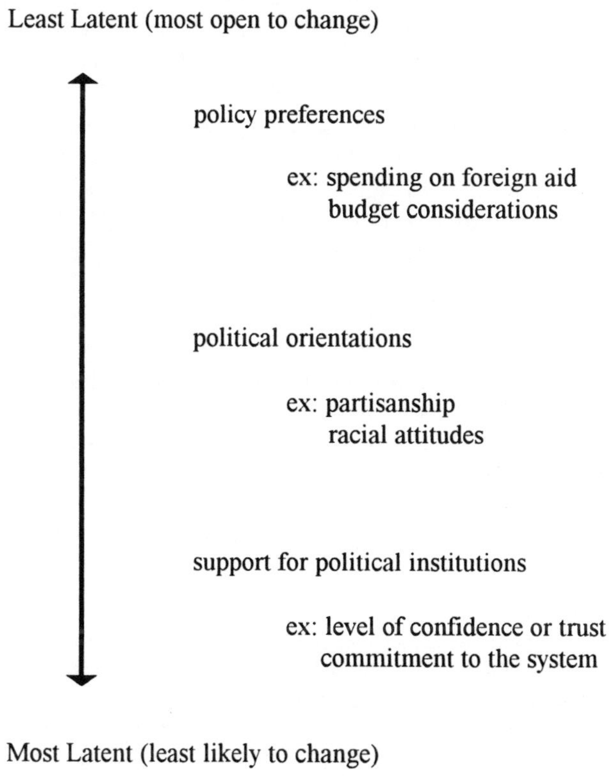

Educating for Democracy

There is a long-standing debate among educators in the United States as to the proper normative role of the schools in educating children about American Government. On one hand, many feel that it is the responsibility of schools to educate for citizenship; that is, to instill the types of values upon which America was founded into children throughout their time in the educational system (see Center for Civic Education 1994). This has been discussed in terms of cultural literacy, education for citizenship, or—to mirror Conover's (1991) distinctions—civic education. On the other hand, there is a movement that stresses the importance of developing critical thinking and analytic skills beyond that which is traditionally discussed in most educational systems.[14] Paulo Freire (1968, chapter 2) differentiates between "banking" and "problem-posing" approaches to education. Banking education is the more traditional and common approach, wherein the instructor "deposits" information into the minds of the students and, at a later time, "withdraws" the information from them (usually in the form of an exam). Alternatively, problem-posing education involves an instructor (or, more appropriately, a "facilitator") asking questions of the students and allowing them to generate answers on their own.[15]

It is important to understand how these two often-competing perspectives are relevant to the formation of political attitudes. If most instructors use the "banking" approach to education, what effect might this have on political learning? It is possible that this approach fosters a normatively positive perception of government at all levels and of all agents. I suspect, however, that the U.S. Supreme Court is presented to students as the defender of the Constitution and the guarantor of civil rights and liberties, while the legislative and executive branches are treated more like "political" branches.[16]

Even as the schools paint positive images of government and governmental leaders in general, the Supreme Court is likely to be portrayed as a unified body (in fact, its members hope that it is perceived as such), not a body composed of individual players, each with his or her own political biases. This lack of "personal" attention allows members of the Court to become less human—less political. If the role of politics on the Court is either ignored or downplayed, the student will be left with a less political impression of the Court than of either of the other two national political institutions.

NOTES

1. See Lenart (1994).

2. Davis (1994) reports the percentage of time each justice's name is mentioned in the period under consideration. I simply added each percentage and divided by the number of justices (eleven) to get the figures I report.

3. *Time* magazine stories especially focused on Justices William Rehnquist and Warren Burger—Burger because of his resignation and chairmanship of the Bicentennial of the Constitution Commission, and Rehnquist because of his new status as Chief

Justice. Thus, there is some reason to suspect that these data are somewhat anomalous in this regard (Davis 1994).

4. This contention is certainly not new. Writers since Plato have acknowledged the necessity for rulers to foster feelings of loyalty and confidence in the regime. Armed with new methodological tools, however, political scientists now had the means to systematically study the components of this phenomenon.

5. While the media increasingly became a field of interest in political science, it was widely considered to be less relevant in the study of early socialization because, at the time, children spent much more time in school and with their families than they did absorbing various media.

6. This is certainly true in the American context but may vary when other nations and political cultures are considered. Easton and Dennis (1969), advocating a higher-level theory of political socialization, note that "[s]ocialization is neither inherently conservatizing nor is it for that matter fundamentally destabilizing. It can contribute to disorder just as it can to peace and harmony, depending on the specific circumstances" (37).

7. While Easton and Dennis (1969) do present some empirical findings, they hurry to point out that these findings are not the primary focus of the study. Rather, they are concerned with articulating a well-defined theory of political socialization.

8. Some work continued to be done on early political socialization, even into the late 1980s. See, for example, Moore, Lare, and Wagner, 1985; and Scarre, 1989.

9. Roberta Sigel (1989) provides an edited volume that further explores adult political socialization.

10. This notion will be tested in the student sample population and discussed in chapter 5.

11. For competing perspectives on this debate, see Hirsch (1993) and Freire (1968). Hirsch emphasizes a substantive body of knowledge that he argues American students ought to know before they leave the public education system. Freire argues for "liberatory" pedagogical practices that allow students to realize their place in the democratic system, thereby strengthening their ability to take rational political action. These authors are merely examples of this multi-faceted discussion; many others have equally compelling and divergent views. Recent work by Anderson et al. (1997), for example, explores teachers' attitudes about citizenship education and commitment to tolerance and diversity.

12. Others promote a more critical approach to citizenship education that allows students to question and ponder their place in a democracy. See, for example, Apple (1993) and Freire (1968).

13. It is most probable, however, particularly given the language of the U.S. Department of Education backed Center for Civic Education (1994), that what students are learning in American Government class is more aligned with Conover's definition of civic education.

14. That is to say that those involved in the critical pedagogy movement recognize that critical thought and analytic skills are thought to be important by most educators. The difference lies in the emphasis on such skills as opposed to information that unequivocally promotes support for the existing political and economic system.

15. Problem-posing education is not the same as the so-called Socratic method (it is not a "method," per se, at all). Socrates did, in fact, ask his students questions, but always to get them to the answer that he wanted. While the practice of having students come to knowledge on their own is similar to liberating pedagogy, the Socratic method

is little more than manipulation of the students' minds to arrive at the same conclusions that might be used with the "banking" approach.

16. Citing Langton and Jennings (1968), among others, Massialas (1972) reminds us that the few empirical studies that do set out to examine the effect of the high school civics curriculum have found no relationship between being enrolled in these courses and political efficacy or participation. He argues that "what appears to be more important than the number of courses offered is whether or not controversial issues are discussed in a classroom climate that is conducive to critical inquiry" (7). Massialas goes on to assert that most textbooks and teachers do not engage in such critical exercises with students. Rather, they are more likely to foster compliance with and obedience toward the existing political structure.

Chapter 3

Adult Support for the U.S. Supreme Court

The Court's authority—possessed of neither the purse nor the sword—
ultimately rests on sustained public confidence in its moral sanction.
—Justice Felix Frankfurter, dissenting in *Baker* v. *Carr* (1962, 267)

Students of the Court have historically struggled to examine support for the
Supreme Court. A large part of the trouble stems from the fact that questions
about the Court are rare and generally not consistent in national survey data.
For an analysis of opinions about the Court over an extended period of time, the
General Social Surveys (GSS) (Davis and Smith 1998) provide the best avail-
able questions. [1]

The question designed to measure confidence in the Supreme Court has been
asked nearly every year the survey has been conducted since 1973. [2] This question occurs in a battery of items asking the respondent to indicate how much
support he or she has for the people running a series of institutions. [3]

There are several strengths of the GSS question for those interested in exam-
ining a general level of support for the Court, rather than support for specific
Court decisions. First, it very broadly asks about level of "confidence" in the
Court, as opposed to asking if the respondent "agrees with" or "approves of" the
Court. Second, the question is virtually the only item about the Supreme Court
in the survey and one of only a fraction of questions directly about politics.
Finally, the question is part of a battery designed to measure confidence in

"institutions" such as banks, the military, medicine, and organized labor—thus the survey does not provide contextual "cues" with issue questions.[4]

John Hibbing and Elizabeth Theiss-Morse (1995) use survey and focus group data to address the issue of evaluating an institution, as opposed to its members. Their results suggest that, for the Court, most people do not differentiate the institution from its members. Both approval and feeling thermometer ratings show lower evaluations of all members as compared to institutions, but the Court has the smallest differential between the two concepts (Hibbing and Theiss-Morse 1995, chapter 3). Further, the authors assert that Americans conceptualize two political systems: constitutional, of which most Americans approve, and a Washington system, of which they are suspect and with which they are generally dissatisfied. Hibbing and Theiss-Morse report that people view both the institution of the Supreme Court and its members as overlapping and lying completely within the constitutional system. In contrast, the presidency is viewed as being within the constitutional system while the president is partly in the Washington system with a strong link between the two. Congress as an institution is seen as lying within the constitutional system, but the members are completely within the Washington system with a weak link between the two (Hibbing and Theiss-Morse 1995, chapter 5). These findings further support the notion that the GSS question about confidence in the people running the Court may actually be measuring a more general level of support for the institution. They suggest also, however, that the GSS questions about the other institutions are merely measuring attitudes about their members.

Perhaps most important, the question on the GSS is the only item about confidence in the Court that has been asked consistently over a significant period of time. All things considered, we can only be confident that the GSS measure captures adult support for "the people running" the Court, keeping in mind that the vast majority of respondents (1) do not know who those people are and (2) do not separate them from the institution.

FINDINGS FROM CROSS-SECTIONAL STUDIES

In the most comprehensive longitudinal analysis of diffuse support for the Court to date, Roger Handberg and William Maddox's (1982) examination of attitudes toward the Court in the 1970s found that party identification and political ideology were less important over the long run.[5] Further, they found that race is significant for nonwhites who grew up during the Warren Court. Education was also found to be significant and positive as it relates to political interest and political socialization; that is, the more education one has, the more likely one is to support the Court. Finally, Handberg and Maddox report that diffuse support is contingent on general support for political institutions. These findings encompass most of the variables that have been found to affect attitudes toward the Court in cross-sectional studies. But the cross-sectional studies are not consistent in their reports of forces influencing attitudes toward and attitude formation about the Court. It is necessary, then, to track trends in attitudes about the Court over time.

Confidence in Other Institutions

Figure 3.1 depicts the percentage of respondents each year who indicated that they had "a great deal" of confidence in the people running each of the three political institutions, while Figure 3.2 shows the trends of those who indicated that they had "hardly any" confidence in them at all.

The Court has, over the last twenty-five years, consistently maintained a sizably higher number of supporters and has kept its "negatives" lower than either of the other two branches.[6] This is not surprising given the low saliency of the Court as compared to the "political" branches: it is easier to have confidence in an institution that is comparatively invisible to the mass public (and, therefore, less criticized).[7] What is interesting, however, is that the ebb and flow of support for the Court moves closely with that of the other branches. This suggests that support for the Court might be related to support for Congress and the executive branch, which is consistent both with Handberg and Maddox's (1982) research, as well as Gregory Caldeira's (1986) where he found that support in the aggregate seemed to move with "events on the political landscape" (1223).

A glance at Figure 3.3 lends further support to this finding by tracking respondents' confidence in the people running the Court in terms of their confidence in members of each of the other two branches of government. Those who have a "great deal" of confidence in either Congress or the executive branch tend to have a lot of confidence in the Court, while those who have minimal confidence in either Congress or the executive also have low confidence in the Court. It appears, then, that Americans evaluate the Court with similar criteria as those they use to evaluate the other two branches.

Party Identification and Ideology

Scholars have disagreed about the roles of party identification and ideology in explaining support for the Court.[8] These two items cannot be expected to impact confidence in the Court in only one direction consistently over the twenty-five-year period. Party identification and political ideology have differing effects on confidence in institutions depending on the political context in which they are measured. Figure 3.4 confirms this notion. No clear trend emerges for any of the four categories of respondents plotted. It is apparent, though, that confidence in the Court waxes and wanes in a similar fashion for Democrats and liberals as it does for Republicans and conservatives.

We can further consider the impact of these attitudes on support for the Court by examining correlations of confidence in each branch with party identification and ideology. Figures 3.5 and 3.6 show graphical illustrations of these correlations over time.

Figure 3.1
Confidence in American Political Institutions (Adults)

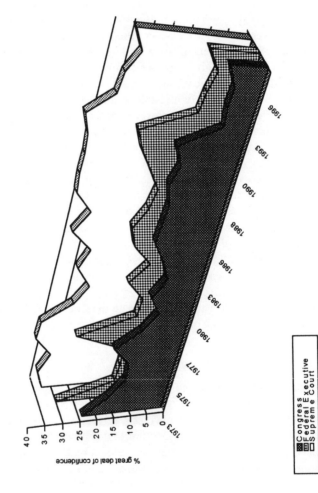

% great deal of confidence

1973 1975 1977 1980 1983 1986 1988 1990 1993 1996

Congress
Federal Executive
Supreme Court

Source: Davis and Smith (1998).

28

Figure 3.2
Lack of Confidence in American Political Institutions (Adults)

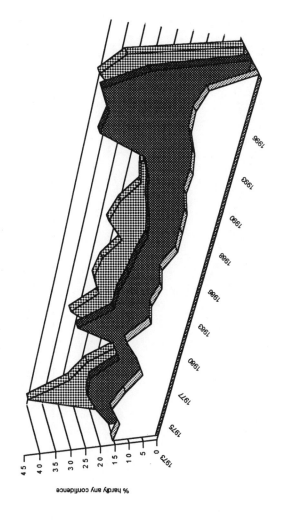

Source: Davis and Smith (1998).

Figure 3.3
Confidence in the Court by Confidence in the Other Branches (Adults)

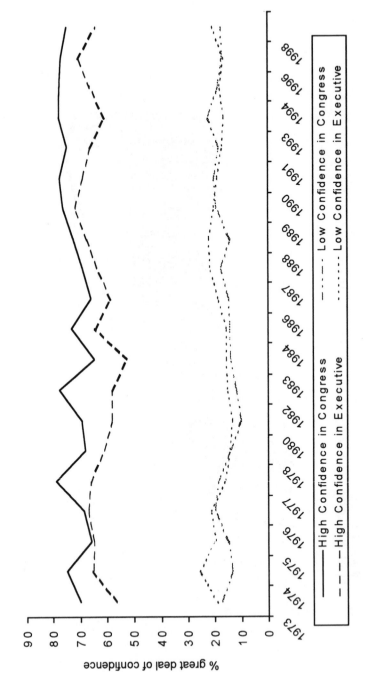

—— High Confidence in Congress	- - - - Low Confidence in Congress	
– – – High Confidence in Executive	· · · · · · Low Confidence in Executive	

Source: Davis and Smith (1998).

It is important to note that none of the correlations ever surpasses .30 or -.30 for party identification, and the range is even smaller for ideology. Little can be substantively interpreted about such weak correlations, but the trends are notable. Perhaps the most interesting story to be told here is that partisanship and ideology matter most to evaluations of the executive branch. The Y-axis moves from negative to positive (Democrat to Republican and liberal to conservative, respectively), and the negative correlations for the executive branch appeared in the seven survey years with Democrat presidents (1977, 1978, 1980, 1993, 1994, 1996, and 1998). This indicates that in those years, Democrats and liberals tended to have more support for the executive branch, and in all other years, Republicans and conservatives had more support for the executive branch (by virtue of the positive correlations).

Confidence in the people running Congress fluctuates more closely about zero, but the lines support intuition. Democrats controlled the House of Representatives during all the years under consideration until 1994, and the Senate during many of the years. In all but four years, the lines for Congress stayed below zero (indicating more support from Democrats and liberals), and in those two years the positive relationship is negligible.

The Supreme Court lines are the least affected by partisanship over this period of time. Its lines fluctuate very closely about zero (suggesting little if any effect of partisanship or ideology), but to the extent that it does move, the more Republican one is, the more trust he or she tends to have in the Court. This may seem logical during the Reagan/Bush years, but in 1993, after Bill Clinton had been elected and the Reagan/Bush years had taken a severe beating during the previous year's election, support for the Court moved in a slightly positive direction (indicating that Republicanism is the cause) while correlations for Congress and the executive dropped dramatically downward (indicating that support for those institutions decreased among Republicans). Perhaps for Republicans, the Court became the last bastion of hope after the 1992 elections. Their party now controlled neither "political" branch of the government, so Republicans, out of necessity, looked to a Court of Republican presidential appointees to carry the torch. Liberals, however, were generally more supportive of the Court than conservatives. So it is liberal-leaning Republicans who tend to have been most supportive of the Court over the last twenty-five years, not ultra-conservatives.

Issues

One of the most compelling academic discussions in judicial support research over the past thirty years has been about the various hypotheses concerning the link between specific support for the Court and diffuse support.[9] Here, I measured attitudes toward Court decisions with items in the GSS that ask respondents to indicate their support for or opposition to various salient social issues. I chose three issues that are both politically salient and linked to the Court: abortion, capital punishment, and school prayer.

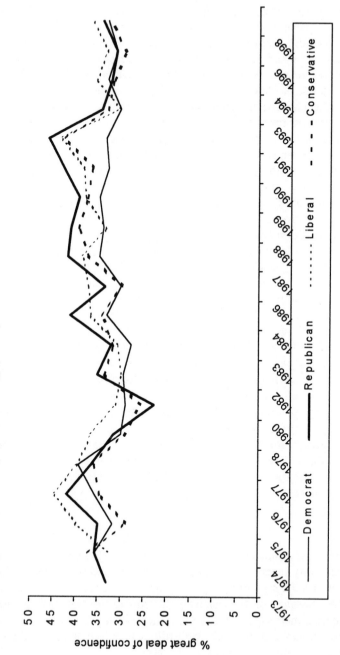

Figure 3.4
Confidence in the Court by Partisanship and Ideology (Adults)

Source: Davis and Smith (1998).

Note: Respondent's party identification and ideology are measured on seven-point scales, where the middle values ("independent" and "moderate," respectively) have been excluded. The remaining values of each scale have been collapsed into the dichotomies presented.

If there are relationships between these variables and confidence in the Court, they should be as follows:

- Those supporting a woman's right to an abortion would have higher confidence in the Court than those who oppose abortion until the late 1980s.[10]
- Those who are in favor of the death penalty for murder should have more confidence in the Court (which declared that capital punishment is not unconstitutional) after the *Gregg* v. *Georgia* decision in 1976.[11]
- Those in favor of prayer in school should be less supportive of the Court than those who oppose school prayer.[12]

Figures 3.7 through 3.9 show confidence in the Court by the respondents' attitudes about abortion, capital punishment, and school prayer respectively. As expected, respondents who are in favor of a woman's right to choose to abort a pregnancy for any reason are more likely to have confidence in the Court than those who oppose abortion. The lines do move somewhat closer together after the late 1980s decisions in *Webster* and *Casey*, but move apart after 1994, possibly due to the fact that Bill Clinton had appointed two rather young justices, making the possibility of overturning *Roe* unlikely.

Respondents who favored capital punishment were less supportive of the Court than those who opposed it until about the mid-1980s. This shift could be a lagged reaction to *Gregg* v. *Georgia* (1976), or a result of the Reagan/Bush appointments. The trend is as predicted over that period of time—those who favor capital punishment for persons convicted of murder are more supportive of the Court (especially when compared to opponents of the death penalty) after the decision in *Gregg*. In 1990s, those who opposed capital punishment were more supportive of the Court than those who supported it. This is perhaps a response to the appointments of Bill Clinton, the first Democrat since Lyndon Johnson to appoint justices to the bench.[13]

Perhaps it is less notable that the school prayer issue generates expected results because the question wording specifically mentions the Supreme Court: "The United States Supreme Court has ruled that no state or local government may require the reading of the Lord's prayer or Bible verses in public schools. What are your views on this—do you approve or disapprove of the court's *[sic]* ruling?" (emphasis in original). Respondents are certainly evaluating their specific support for this particular Court decision (presumably *Abbington School District* v. *Schempp*).

Race

The literature has been quite consistent about the impact of race on attitudes toward the Court: nonwhites are generally less supportive than whites.[14] Figure 3.10 presents confidence in the people running the Supreme Court by race. While the lines move together for the most part, white support is generally higher than nonwhite support.

Figure 3.5
Correlation of Party Identification and Confidence in Political Institutions (Adults)

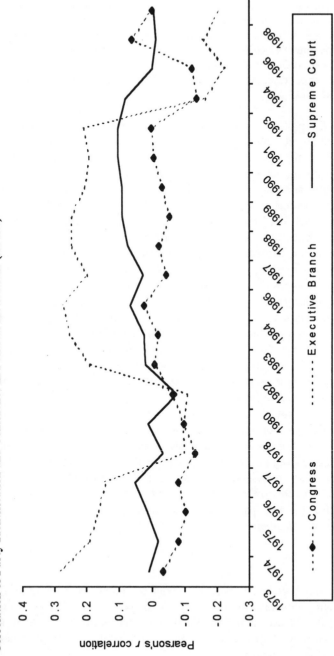

Source: Davis and Smith (1998).

Note: Confidence in each institution is measured on a three-point scale that has been coded so that higher values indicate more confidence in the people running the institution. Party identification is measured on a seven-point scale that has been coded so that higher values indicate that the respondent is Republican.

34

Figure 3.6
Correlation of Ideology and Confidence in Political Institutions (Adults)

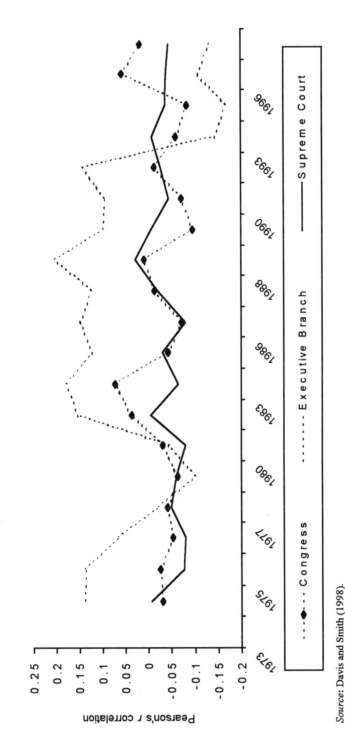

Source: Davis and Smith (1998).

Note: Confidence in each institution is measured on a three-point scale that has been coded so that higher values indicate more confidence in the people running the institution. Ideology is measured on a seven-point scale that has been coded so that higher values indicate that the respondent is conservative.

Figure 3.7
Confidence in the Court and Attitudes about Abortion (Adults)

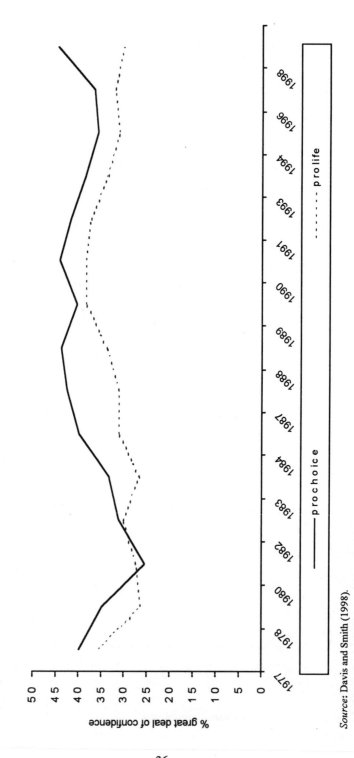

Source: Davis and Smith (1998).

36

Figure 3.8
Confidence in the Court and Attitudes about Capital Punishment (Adults)

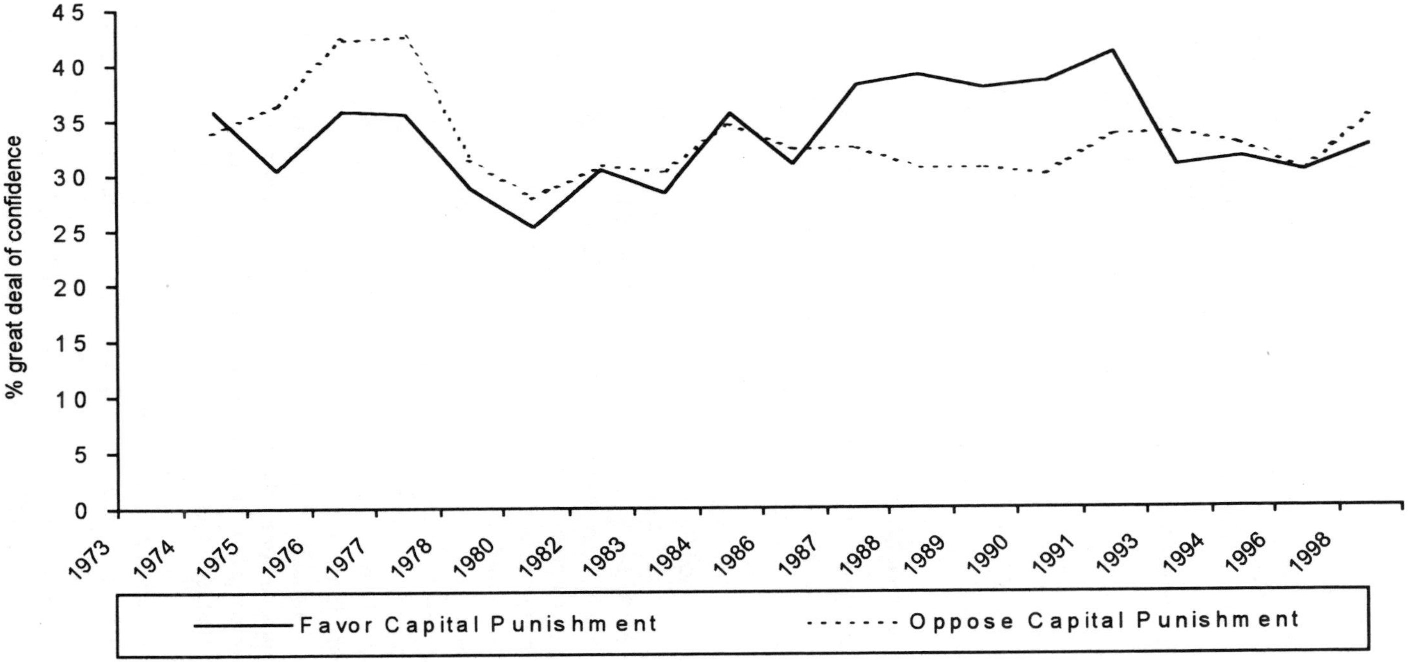

Source: Davis and Smith (1998).

Education

Handberg and Maddox (1982) found education to be the most important predictor of trust in the Court, noting that the more educated had more trust in the Court due to their ability to "observe and assess the Court with at least a more generalized frame of reference" (345). Figure 3.11 shows confidence in the Court by level of education. Confidence is generally greater as one increases his or her level of education. It is notable that there is considerably more fluctuation in support for the Court among the most highly educated in the sample. These "opinion leaders" are perhaps, as Caldeira and Gibson (1992) found, most likely to evaluate the Court based on its decisions. As one's level of education decreases, the lines smooth out, indicating that there is less fluctuation among respondents in that group from year to year. This is the real base of the Court's diffuse support. Accordingly, it is the education system to which we must turn to get a better picture of how this adult support is derived.

Political Socialization

Herbert Hyman (1959) argued that political behavior is a result of learning that begins in early childhood and is completed, for the most part, in adolescence. The 1960s and 1970s saw a slew of studies aimed at understanding political socialization. This work was primarily concerned with what information children and adolescents receive and how that information impacts political attitudes into adulthood.[15]

The Supreme Court has enjoyed a rather symbolic place in the minds of Americans by being considered a sort of defender of the Constitution. Removed from the day-to-day political association in the media, the Court is only portrayed as a political institution in two situations: during confirmation hearings of nominees and when it rules on a particularly salient and controversial issue. Accordingly, there is reason to suspect that those socialized during the more active Courts of Earl Warren may have different attitudes about the Court than those socialized during "quieter" Courts. It is possible to test this hypothesis by creating a dummy variable for "Warren Court socialization."[16]

Figure 3.12 shows the percentage of all respondents who had a great deal of confidence in the Court by cohort. On the whole, those socialized during the Warren Court tend to have less confidence in the Court than those socialized at other times, although the difference is not particularly striking. If Americans who learned about the Court during the Warren years are, because of that Court's activism, more likely to consider the Court a political institution than those who were socialized during more politically quiet Courts, they may have a tendency not to hold the Court in quite as high regard as others do.

Having been socialized during the Warren Court may particularly have an impact on confidence in the Court when mediated by race, as the salient decisions made by the Warren Court effectively helped to advance the cause of the civil rights movement.[17] It would be expected that nonwhites socialized during

Figure 3.9
Confidence in the Court and Attitudes about Mandatory Prayer in School (Adults)

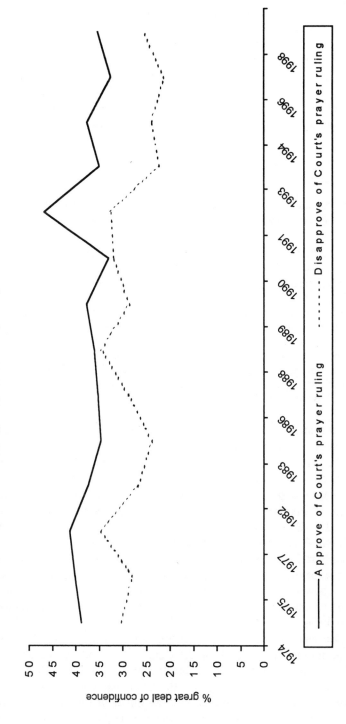

Source: Davis and Smith (1998).

Note: The school prayer question was asked only sporadically between 1975 and 1988.

the Warren Court would have more confidence in the Court than either whites socialized during the Warren Court or nonwhites socialized at other periods of time. Figures 3.13 and 3.14 graphically represent the effects of belonging to the Warren Court cohort by race. The sample of white respondents (Figure 3.13) depicts a very similar picture to Figure 3.12 (the entire sample), while Figure 3.14 is less clear. For the most part, nonwhite support for the Court is greater among those socialized outside of the Warren Court years.[18]   This leaves us with no clear indication about the effect of socialization on support for the Court.

DISCUSSION

When respondents were asked if members of American political institutions triggered certain emotions, they answered as follows:

- 7 per cent said that members of the Court made them feel most *angry* (as compared to 30 per cent for the president and 60per cent for members of Congress);
- 7per cent reported feeling most *disgusted* with members of the Court (as opposed to 32 per cent for the president and 61 per cent for members of Congress);
- 24per cent felt that members of the Court made them most *afraid* (32 per cent for the president and 45 per cent for members of Congress);
- 20 per cent reported feeling most *uneasy* about members of the Court (32 per cent for the president and 48 per cent for members of Congress); and
- 35 per cent said that members of the Court made them feel the most *proud* (as opposed to 51 per cent for the president and 14 per cent for Congress) (Hibbing and Theiss-Morse 1995, 57-58).

While it is apparent that the Court need not be concerned with the same level of distrust that plagues Congress, neither does the Court have the luxury of meaningful participation amidst widespread contempt. But as Jeffery Mondak and Shannon Ishiyama Smithey (1997) note: "a system can be stable in the ag-gregate despite a great deal of individual-level change" (23). They point out further that "aggregate stability need not be the product of individual-level in-activity" (29). Rather, if an institution maintains the "reservoir of good will" of which David Easton writes, it will persevere in a democratic system even if it occasionally makes policy that is contrary to popular sentiment. This seems to be the case for the Supreme Court. While people may disagree with particular decisions (however salient), their commitment to the constitutionality they view the Court as embodying allows them to "forgive" specific disagreements and maintain diffuse support for the Court.[19]

Attitudes about the other two branches of government seem to be most heav-ily responsible for attitudes about the Court. But while movement in confi-dence in members of Congress and the executive coincides with movement in confidence in members of the Court, the Court has consistently been able to maintain a higher level of confidence than either of the other two branches. Further, Figures 3.5 and 3.6 indicate that people do differentiate between the

Figure 3.10
Confidence in the Court by Race (Adults)

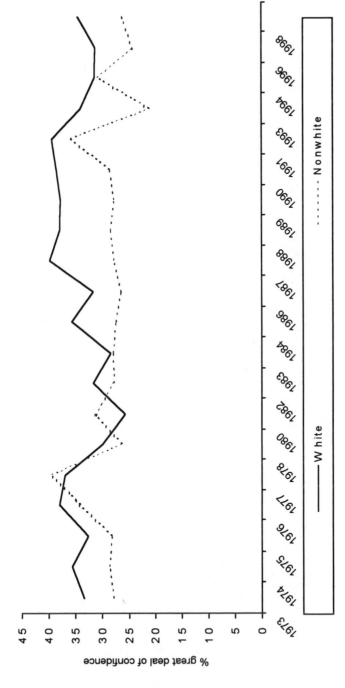

Source: Davis and Smith (1998).

Note: Race has been recoded into a dichotomous variable.

Figure 3.11
Confidence in the Court by Education (Adults)

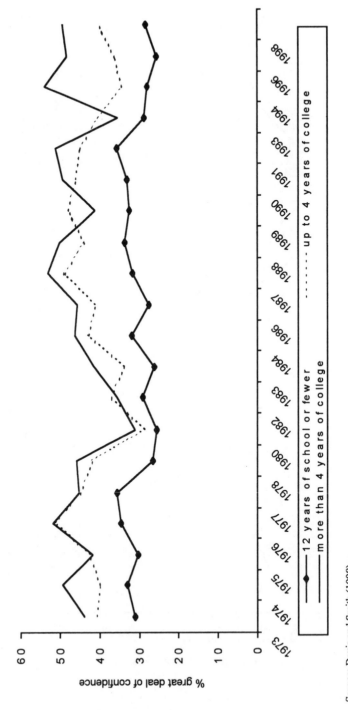

% great deal of confidence

12 years of school or fewer
up to 4 years of college
more than 4 years of college

Source: Davis and Smith (1998).

Note: Education has been collapsed into a three-point scale.

Figure 3.12
Confidence in the Court by Socialization Cohort (Adults)

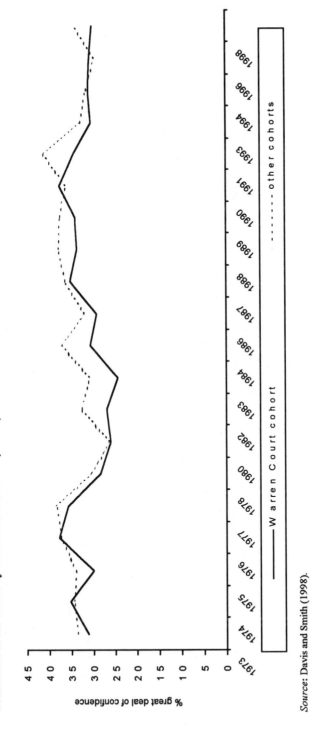

Source: Davis and Smith (1998).

Note: Respondents born between 1933 and 1953 are considered to be members of the Warren Court socialization cohort.

43

Figure 3.13
Confidence in the Court by Race and Socialization Cohort: Whites (Adults)

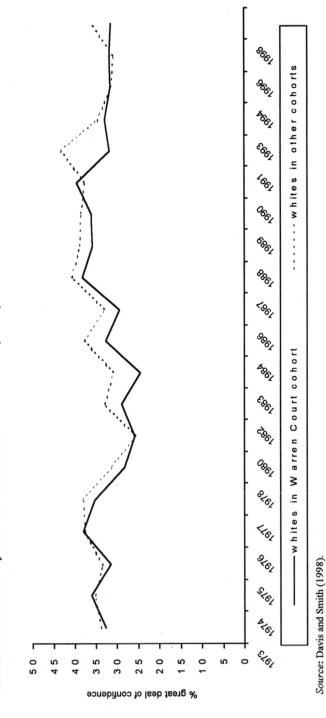

Source: Davis and Smith (1998).

Note: Respondents born between 1933 and 1953 are considered to be members of the Warren Court socialization cohort. Race has been recoded into a dichotomous variable.

Figure 3.14
Confidence in the Court by Race and Socialization Cohort: Non-whites (Adults)

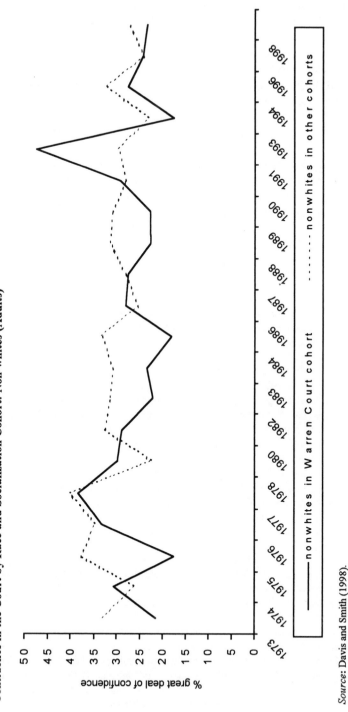

Source: Davis and Smith (1998).

Note: Respondents born between 1933 and 1953 are considered to be members of the Warren Court socialization cohort. Race has been recoded into a dichotomous variable.

branches of government, and evaluate them partially as a function of their partisanship and/or ideology. It is not possible to tell from these data precisely why the Court has been able to maintain greater support than Congress or the executive. According to Hibbing and Theiss-Morse (1995), Americans do not generally think of the Court as dealing with the nation's most important problems (49). If this is so, we can surmise that the Court is less likely to be blamed as much as the other two branches when people are dissatisfied with government. So while confidence in the Court changes as confidence in the members of the other branches change, attitudes about certain salient issues and one's level of education also have an effect on the Court's level of support.[20] As Handberg and Maddox (1982) note in their study of the 1970s, "no simple set of variables appears to explain variations in evaluations [of the Court]" (345). We are still a long way from explaining why people hold the Court in higher confidence than either of the other two branches, and more work needs to be done to that end. In the following chapters, attention is paid to political education as an explanatory construct.

NOTES

1. General Social Surveys, 1972-1998 cumulative file are collected at the National Opinion Research Center at the University of Chicago (ICPSR# 2685).

2. The question was not asked in 1985, and since 1988 it has only been asked to two-thirds of the respondents.

3. When I first examined this question, I expected that it would be a good indicator of diffuse support for the Court. After all, a 1989 *Washington Post* poll reported that 71 per cent of the American public could not name any of the current justices of the Court (cited in Epstein et al. 1994, 609). To test whether the GSS question is, indeed, a good measure of diffuse support, I included it in a pilot study of college students. Respondents were asked both the GSS question and the items in the diffuse support scale used by Caldeira and Gibson (1992) (the exact wording of the questions appears in the Appendix). There is a statistically significant, but low, Pearson's r correlation between the GSS item and the diffuse support scale (.258). While the population of the pilot study does not allow me to draw any definite conclusions about the relationship between the two measures, there is at least reason to suspect that there is some substantive difference. Hibbing and Theiss-Morse (1995) report, however, that "[focus group] comments on the Supreme Court justices . . . were highly unusual. Most participants, when they talked about the Court at all, focused on its institutional aspect, not on the people who constitute it" (95). This suggests that, unlike Congress, people do not commonly think of the Court as a sum of its members.

4. In fact, just as the GSS question does not correlate highly with the diffuse support scale, neither does it correlate highly with a factor of specific support generated by responses to three questions on my undergraduate survey about agreement or disagreement with salient Court rulings (Pearson's $r = .260$, $p < .01$).

5. This is contrary to earlier studies by Dolbeare and Hammond (1968), Tanenhaus and Murphy (1981), and Casey (1976). Mishler and Sheehan (1993) also conducted a longitudinal analysis on attitudes toward the Court, but they were concerned with whether or not public opinion influences the way the Court decides issues. They found

that at a time lag, the public mood affects Court decisions and that the Court's decisions also affect the public mood.

6. This is consistent with Mondak and Smithey's (1997) finding that "aggregate support for the Supreme Court is stable and high" (1119).

7. In fact, Hibbing and Theiss-Morse (1995) found that respondents placed the Supreme Court closest to themselves ideologically, despite the fact that the Court is the furthest removed from them politically. It was Congress, the supposed institution of the people, that they viewed as being farthest from themselves ideologically.

8. Dolbeare and Hammond (1968) found that party identification was related to support for the Court while Casey (1976) and Tanenhaus and Murphy (1981) found that ideology was a better indicator. Handberg and Maddox (1982) found that neither was very important in determining support for the Court.

9. Caldeira and Gibson (1992) found no relationship between these two concepts among the mass public in 1987. They did, however, find some relationship among "opinion leaders."

10. Cases such as *Webster* v. *Reproductive Health Services* (1989) and *Planned Parenthood of Southeastern Pennsylvania* v. *Casey* (1992) will likely make the effect of abortion attitudes on support for the Court less clear.

11. Before then, *Furman* v. *Georgia* (1972) was the law of the land, and all state capital punishment laws were struck down.

12. While the Court has made allowances for release time, it has ruled against both broadcast Bible readings (*Abbington School District* v. *Schempp* 1963) and mandatory moments of silence (*Wallace* v. *Jaffree* 1985; *Lee* v. *Weissman* 1992). For a discussion of the ways in which schools have circumvented the release time decision in *Zorach* v. *Clauson* (1952), see Sorauf (1959).

13. This is not a logical rationale, however, since Bill Clinton is not an opponent of capital punishment.

14. See Gibson and Caldeira (1992); Handberg and Maddox (1982); Secret, Johnson, and Welch (1986); and Sigelman (1979). Some work has shown blacks to be more favorable toward the Court (Hirsch and Donohew 1968), but it was largely a function of the Warren Court's activism in civil rights cases (see Sigelman 1979).

15. For discussion of political socialization among adults, see, among others, Sigel (1989).

16. In this study, the Warren Court cohort is composed of respondents who were born between 1933 and 1953.

17. See Gibson and Caldeira (1992).

18. Consistent with Gibson and Caldeira (1992), though, one of the times Warren Court cohort support was greater was around 1986 and 1987—the time when the data in their study were collected.

19. Mondak and Smithey (1997) propose an empirically grounded theoretical model that indicates that "the Court would enter precarious turf only if it were to rule against the tide of public opinion at an extremely frequent rate" (1131).

20. These findings are consistent with much of the extant literature on public opinion toward the Court, but confirm that the findings hold over a twenty-five-year period of time, indicating further that the attitudes and characteristics that are responsible for feelings about the Court are as stable as feelings about the Court themselves.

Chapter 4

In Their Own Words: Teachers on Teaching

> I guess what I'm always looking to do is to show my enthusiasm for government, for politics, for history because I really love it. I mean, that's my job and it's my hobby. I mean, when I have spare time I'm doing that—reading about politics and history and that sort of thing.
>
> —Mr. Caballero

Byron Massialas (1972) argues that the content of the course is most significant to a student's political education. If it is designed in such a way as to allow students to engage in critical discussion and inquiry, students learn that it is permissible to question the political system. If, on the other hand, teachers subscribe to what Paulo Freire (1968) calls the "banking concept" of education (where teachers "deposit" knowledge into students, only to "withdraw" it later on an exam), noncritical support for the existing political system and its institutions is more likely to exist.

This chapter examines teachers' attitudes about teaching in general and, more specifically, teaching American Government (and the Supreme Court). Are teachers striving to educate primarily from a bias toward the American political system (as one might expect), or are they fostering critical thinking about the system? Do they allow their own political beliefs to become the basis of the course? How much do teachers rely on the course textbook? How do individual teachers' attitudes and approaches differ from one another? All of the teachers' names have been changed, as anonymity was promised to all participants.

DIFFERENCES AMONG TEACHERS

In order to determine whether or not political socialization matters with respect to how students feel about the Supreme Court, it is necessary to have some variance in the way students learn about politics, and specifically the Court. Fortunately, the five teachers in this study vary considerably in their age, experience, and philosophy of teaching.[1] This chapter explores the similarities and differences of these five instructors.

PROFILES

Table 4.1 shows the education, experience, salary, and textbook usage of each teacher in the study. While they all possess a master's degree, only two have advanced degrees in their substantive area: the Catholic school teacher (Mr. Caballero) has a master's degree in political science, and Mr. Peralta has a master's in history, although he was unclear as to whether his master's was in education and in history, or in education with a concentration in history.[2] Salaries are competitive with one another among public school teachers. All of the school districts that had decided on a textbook for 1997-2003 were changing from that which they had been using the previous six years.[3]

To allow the reader to get to know the teachers as individuals, I want to describe them both in terms of my observations and, as the chapter is titled, in their own words. I could not have asked for a more philosophically diverse and interesting group of teachers for this study. They varied with respect to their experience, their approaches to teaching, and, perhaps most notably, their personalities. My intent is for this chapter to address both similarities and differences among the teachers within the parameters of the questions at hand. I will start with a brief description of each teacher before moving to specific attitudes and characteristics.

Mr. Kaupas has twenty-six years of experience and is teaching at a rural high school. He describes his reputation with students this way:

Well, I probably think, over the years when I first came here, of course, it takes you a while to build up a reputation. I would think that most of my—it kind of gets handed down from one class to the next. . . . Government class isn't easy. That you better pay attention. . . . And, probably, I think they kind of perceive it, not necessarily, probably pretty strict in a sense, but yet pretty . . . that they're going to have somewhat of a good time or something. That I have a sense of humor and that I try to let them have a sense of humor and it's not always, you know, every second of the day is on the time and the task, dedicated to the subject matter every second. . . . So I guess, I don't know, I guess I'm considered maybe somewhat of a semi-tough class to get through but something that you can do if you just put, if you take the time. And, I don't know, I'm not above calling somebody out in class if I see behavior that I don't like, and some teachers just won't like do that at all, it's not politically correct, and I think that word spreads out real quick.

He is proud of not being "politically correct" and often expresses his frustration with "flavor-of-the-day" teaching techniques and what he consideres to be the hypersensitivity of some of his colleagues. In this way, Mr. Kaupas might be described as "old school," but such a characterization would only be partially correct. The fact is that the students like him. They like him partially because he is personable and casual in class, and, I suspect, partially because he is not the most academically demanding teacher. As we will see below, much of class time every day is spent on small talk with students (even when there was a visitor in the room), so the students see the class as being somewhat of a break in their day. When it is time to get down to business, Mr. Kaupas does most of the talking (as he readily admits), so students do not, necessarily, have to be prepared to come to class. This is a stark contrast to the level of preparedness Mr. Caballero expects.

Teaching in a Catholic school, Mr. Caballero certainly enjoys, on average, a different level of motivation among his students than do the public school teachers. He estimates that approximately 10 per cent of his students will struggle in his class—a number significantly lower than any of the public school teachers would be able to offer. The proportion of parents who are actively involved in their child's education, as opposed to those who are not, is higher due at least partly to the fact that the parents are paying to send their children to school. The youngest teacher in the study, he is interested in serving as a catalyst for thought:

So, you know, I really focus in on hopefully providing them with a set of questions or concepts that they can take out of the classroom, because I know that they're not going to remember 95 per cent of the stuff that we go over in class. So if we can kind of focus on a few concepts that they will remember and that they get practice applying as they read the newspaper and as we talk about some articles in class . . . hopefully, they'll hear me saying, you know, "What is the political, social, and economic aspects of this? What groups are involved?" That kind of thing.

But merely fostering thought, though, does not mean *critical* thought. As numerous as the constraints are in a public school, parochial schools have their own set of limitations on teachers and students. This fact does more to frustrate a teacher like Mr. Caballero than it would a teacher like Mr. Kaupas, since the former has the energy, the drive, and, perhaps most important, the students to engage in controversial discussion day after day. Nonetheless, Mr. Caballero understands his role, and so expresses his goals:

I guess my number one thing I want to show them is that, you know, show the enthusiasm that I have for it, and more generally to show the value of education and try to convey to them that it is important even if they don't recognize—and they don't recognize at this stage—that it's important, but, you know, I'm hoping that they'll see me as someone who is knowledgeable about a lot of things, not just about politics, but we talk about a lot of different things.

Table 4.1
Government Teachers' Experience and Textbook Preferences

Teacher	Degree/Major	Years Teaching	Salary	Current Textbook	New Textbook
Mr. Kaupas	Bachelor's/Political Science Master's/Education	26	$42,395	Turner, *et al.*	Remy
Mr. Caballero	Bachelor's/Political Science Master's/Political Science	9	$27,010 (est.)	Remy	Undecided
Mr. Hawk	Bachelor's/Political Science Master's/Education & U.S. History	36	$43,766	Turner, *et al.*	Magruder's
Mr. Peralta	Bachelor's/Physical Education Master's/Education	35	$43,766	Turner, *et al.*	Magruder's
Mr. McGill	Bachelor's/Education Master's/Education	13	$37,214	Turner, *et al.*	Magruder's

Note: Mr. Caballero's salary was not publicly available since he works at a private school. During his interview, he mentioned that the school was trying to get all the teachers up to 75 per cent of the local public schools. Accordingly, his salary is estimated by figuring 75 per cent of what his salary would be in a public school with nine years of experience.

My experience in his class was that he is, indeed, meeting his goals. Students show him a great deal of respect, but seem very comfortable in his class. He receives the most participation of any teacher in the study (the students' talent may account for this as well). His students will remember the classroom discussions, even if his fears are realized and they do not remember the content.

Students of Mr. Hawk (now deceased) will certainly have a less memorable class experience. Thirty-six years of experience did not diminish his enthusiasm for teaching, but he lost the ability to reach students and hold their interest in class. To the students, the course became little more than an unpleasant necessity that they must endure in order to graduate. They came into his class expecting the worst. He was aware of this problem, and spoke to me about how he felt about it:

Well, you know, the reputation that I have . . . is that my class is a rough class. And a lot of kids come back and say, "Oh thanks. You really prepared me for college" and stuff like that. A lot of kids could care less about that stuff. But what's developed over the years is that they've seemed to develop a fear, and that's what bothers me, because—even among some parents—you know, they say, "well we've heard this and we've heard that and it really worries us," and so forth. And I'd like to knock that fear part out.

He never got a chance to do that, as he passed away in late June 1997. The viewing before his funeral was a rather jovial gathering of former students and colleagues, all talking and remembering the person above the teacher. But Mr. Hawk loved teaching and he was the consummate professional, always wearing a tie to work and taking care of the administrative tasks around the department. Still, the current and former students with whom I spoke about Mr. Hawk had few nice words to offer about his class. He was tough, and apparently not bashful about failing students—a trait not likely to make one popular when one is teaching a mandatory course for seniors.

Mr. Peralta similarly has a great deal of experience (thirty-five years) but has a teaching style quite different from that of Mr. Hawk. Where Mr. Hawk spoke so softly in class that I could barely hear at times (many students were sleeping or writing notes to friends anyway), Mr. Peralta projects his voice and is extremely demonstrative during his lectures. And he does lecture almost exclusively. As his colleague. Mr. McGill was quick to note, Mr. Peralta has a clear mission: to sell democracy to his students. During our interview, he reiterated several times that he views himself as a "salesman for democracy," a concept he defines this way:

There are not a high percent of people in the United States that are true believers from the standpoint that they can do this, and this is what I tell students: to be a true believer in the democratic way of life, what you have to do is to be able to not just tolerate, but whole-heartedly support the rights of others to do things you personally find disgusting. I mean disgusting in the "oh, God it makes me sick to think about it" [sense]. But, since it's not a threat to my life, liberty or property, it's not a threat to the system, the ideal is that they be allowed to do that. And students, naturally, like most people, think, "now wait a minute. I don't know." See, and I try to point out the advantages. Like, "wait a minute. You don't do it because you like those people. You can dislike them and still support their right to do those things because you're going to benefit. Because if you do that for them, they'll probably do the same thing for you. So you enhance your own freedom by supporting people's rights to do things you personally find disgusting.

I pushed him to think about his role as a teacher more generally, hoping that he would explain his pedagogical tendencies. But, instead, he continued to explain why it is necessary to sell the concept of democracy, juxtaposing his approach to what he viewed as the prevailing practice:

[My role is in] promoting the democratic way of life. Selling people on the democratic way of life. And, someone earlier today said it's important that they know who their senators are and I said, "I don't think so." That doesn't mean you understand the democratic way of life because you understand who your two United States Senators are or who your state representative is. I think it's okay that you know it, but you don't have to know that to understand democracy because those things, those people are changing all the time. . . . It doesn't mean you understand, appreciate or respect the democratic way of life because you know who they are. I mean they're changing all the time anyway, so I'm trying to sell the system—the basic concepts and principles for which democracy is designed to operate.

Like Mr. Hawk, though, a sizable number of students fail Mr. Peralta's class each year. When that happens during the first half of the year, students are forced to take the class again, this time with the other Government teacher, Mr. McGill.

If Mr. Peralta focuses primarily on the conceptual aspects of the democratic way of life, Mr. McGill is 180 degrees in the opposite direction in terms of his goals:

I think they need to know how state and local government works. That's the part of government they're going to be dealing with the rest of their lives. You know, I'm not a Bill Clinton fan, but Bill Clinton in the White House has not caused my lifestyle to change one bit. Whereas local property taxes, local ordinances, you know, who the county commissioners are, decisions that they make, you know, whether I'm in the county or I get annexed in the city, where my kids are going to school . . . yeah, those guys are—that is a very strong daily impact. I think the kids need to know that.

Mr. McGill is a cynic by nature. He takes a very matter-of-fact tone with both students and colleagues, cracking dry jokes with no smile. When asked what section of the textbook is most likely to be left out, he replied "the comparative world governments. . . . I think we're past that." He added:

The Cold War is over and I think everybody, you know, there's not too many of these kids that are worried about, you know, communists taking over the world. I think we can probably do without that.

This teacher likes the nuts and bolts. He approaches teaching wholly from a utilitarian perspective, looking for information students will be able to "use" or that will make a difference in their lives.[4] He concluded our interview by suggesting an overhaul of the Government curriculum to require visits to local government agencies (the county courthouse, for example) and a greater percentage of time spent on state and local government. Despite this passionate call for reform, Mr. McGill spent the bulk of time during my visits sitting behind his desk reading the paper or using his computer while the students either watched a movie or worked on assignments at their seats. Most small talk centered around high school sports. The fact that I could tell which students the teacher coached (even though it was not football season) is illustrative of the way he related to them, as compared to the others.

COACHING AND PRIORITIES

Besides teaching, many teachers have other responsibilities at school. These duties range from parking lot patrol (Mr. Peralta) to director of technology (Mr. Caballero), and include coaching interscholastic athletic teams. This duty has come to symbolize a trend in social studies education.

In fact, it has become almost cliché to suggest that many high school social studies teachers are there because schools need some place to put the coaches. The reality, however, does not much differ from the lore. Of these five teachers, two are currently coaching (Mr. Kaupas and Mr. McGill), one has coached in the past (Mr. Peralta), and another had been involved in other capacities with sports programs at the school (Mr. Hawk). It would be unfair to conclude that these teachers are less qualified to teach Government because they coach, but one might surmise that the academic subject might not be their first priority. The one teacher who has no interest or history in school sports laments the fact that so many of his colleagues are so chosen:

Well, I guess I just feel like—Government, especially Government, tends to get shoved off on coaches and lousy teachers and I think that kids just have—and I mean that's going to be it. When you have them in public school for maybe a year of civics as freshmen and a semester as seniors, that's it. That's it for citizenship training. . . . And I've talked to coaches and they say, "Hey, I'm not going to get another job because I'm a good teacher, I'm going to get another job because I'm a good coach, so that's what I'm putting my energy into." And frankly, I'm not sure I can get another job outside of this school because I'm *not* a coach. . . . I just think that we do a real disservice by tending to make social science and social studies the dumping ground for coaches. (Mr. Caballero)

His comments suggest that the two teachers who are currently coaching may not be giving very careful attention to teaching Government. This would not come out in their conversations with me, of course, since they knew my interest in them was academic.

Indeed, Mr. Caballero has an acute understanding of what goes on in public school Government classes in his area. Directly after he made the above comments, he added:

And one other thing. The kids, they never get a minute of free time in this class, not a minute. It's bell to bell. And I can't imagine how anyone can do it, teach Government in a semester, because I have a whole year, and I'm struggling now. I'm down to the end and we're cramming in Government and Economy. . . . I mean—how can you only get them for one semester and say, "alright, you are trained to go out and be an informed citizen?"

All four of the other teachers, from my observations and their own admission, routinely give students the last five, ten, even fifteen minutes of the forty-eight minute class to "do as they please." This is often justified by the fact that one of the other sections was falling behind, or that they should be doing homework during that time. Mr. Peralta allowed students to get parts of his newspapers to read during the free time, but, as one might expect, the sports section usually went first, leaving the other parts still on his desk. Nonetheless, no teacher claimed to have enough time to cover the material in the textbook in a given semester.

Despite this lack of careful concern for time, I did not get the sense that any of the teachers were necessarily incompetent to teach Government in an informative sense to high school students. Whether there is any deep commitment to helping students to understand the less concrete areas of the American political system (and the students' places in it) remains to be determined. The rest of this chapter is devoted to the exploration of this question.

EDUCATING FOR CITIZENSHIP

The Center for Civic Education (1994) asserts that "formal instruction in civics and government should provide students with a basic understanding of civic life, politics, and government" (1). While this is a short sentence, it is a tall task to ask of teachers, especially in one semester. Accordingly, teachers take different approaches to their responsibility of educating these young citizens to be able participants in the democratic process.

Most of the teachers are interested primarily in generating some level of interest in their students. They perceive the students as being content with remaining relatively isolated from the rest of the world. As Mr. Hawk put it, "[I want] to create an awareness of what's going on, you know, we're not living in a little box. . . . So many of those kids lack awareness, have no idea, and I think that Government [class] should make them aware of what is going on in government . . . so I would just say 'awareness.' " Some teachers go a step further and attempt to convince students of their importance in the democratic system:

I'd like to have them feel that somewhat there can be, they can have some kind of influence on the process. I mean, that sounds kind of corny, but, maybe, they think that, you know, first of all, you get them to kind of realize what's going on out there, you know, and then to feel that they can have some—not that they can totally structure policy, that they can be aware of what is going on. Just to be, if they could just like read the news-paper or watch the news, make some halfway, be able to make some halfway intelligent observations and judgments and decisions, rather than there just being this body of knowledge out there that goes on that they're totally, feel totally separated from. That's kind of, because I really think the chances of you inspiring some young student to be a politician are probably pretty minimal, but if they can feel like this process and this whole thing, they can be a part of it, they can be somewhat politically effective, that's kind of—what I want them to be able to think. And maybe take away some of the mys-tery and the hocus pocus about it, and that there's this thing called—whether it be the legislative branch or the presidency or how we pick a president—and kind of make it more simplistic, okay. And make it less, you know, more understandable. (Mr. Kau-pas)

In the second sentence of the passage, he quickly backs off what appeared to be a statement advocating student empowerment. He says that the students should "feel that they can have some—" and then quickly backpedals to change the goal to merely "being aware of what is going on." His rhetoric follows closely to what the Center for Civic Education calls for in terms of "enabl[ing] students to learn how to participate in their own governance" (1994, 1). But it is un-clear as to whether or not this feeling of empowerment (assuming for a moment that the teachers are successful) translates into support for or cynicism about the political system.

In some cases, the answer is clear. Mr. Peralta, for instance, is adamant about his role as a Government instructor: "Well, I'm trying to sell democracy. See, because I became sold on it. As a result of teaching, I began looking and thinking and I thought, 'hey—' . . . I got sold on it because I started seeing the benefits. You know, personal benefits. And so, I try to sell students on it. I mean, I guess I see myself as a salesman." This teacher got into Government through the back door. As a young teacher certified in physical education and health,[5] he was asked to cover Government one year since he had more hours of Government courses than any of the other social studies teachers at the school. But then came a revelation: "I really started liking it." Listening to him talk about his being "sold" conjures images of fundamentalist Christians espousing their duty to "save" as many others as they can. Using words like "devout" and "believers," Mr. Peralta takes a spirited approach to teaching his students about democratic ideals:

If you look at the concepts and the principles, boy, it's a great way of life if you can sell people on it. Problem is that we don't have still a lot of people sold on it. I mean there are a lot of people who are somewhat believers, but not true believers. . . . So I'm trying to sell them [the students] on the democratic way of life because I became sold on it. And I think you can be a pretty effective salesperson if you are sold. I'm not sure you'll be very effective selling me some shoes if you're not sold on the shoes. If you're a be-liever of going barefoot, I think it's probably hard for you to sell me shoes. But if you are a devout believer in shoes, you might be able to sell me shoes when I wasn't sure I wanted them. And that's what I'm trying to do, I'm trying to sell them on the democratic way of life.

Conover (1991) would call this kind of political learning "civic education" since it obviously promotes support for the existing regime.[6] Mr. Caballero takes a similar position, saying that he sees himself as "a trainer for democracy" who tries to provide students with "the tools that allow them to make good decisions in voting and just deciding where they stand on issues." But he is not often critical of the system.[7] This can be contrasted with the approach Mr. McGill takes to transmitting political information, which might best be described as critical, at least in the colloquial sense of the word. When asked what his teaching goals are, he responded as follows:

It's important to me that these kids think. That they learn to start making valued judgments based on the facts rather than, you know, their emotions. Try to be independent, you know, mom and dad have decided whether you are a Republican or Democrat to this point. I try to tell the kids, "make up your own minds." The first day of class when I have seniors, I say, "you know, for the last twelve years you guys have been [told] what to do, how to do it, what it is to do, sometimes why, sometimes how, but you people need to start making your own decisions."

He echoes Mr. Hawk's sentiments about students not knowing about a world outside their hometown when he explains how he helps students to become thoughtful about their environment: "I encourage the kids to read. I don't care if they read *Sports Illustrated* or *Vanity Fair* or *Redbook*, *Playboy*, whatever. You know, I want them to read. To realize there's more out there than [their local] county. Unfortunately most of the kids in my class are going to be here until the day they die." He "encourages the kids to argue" and does not "get upset when somebody argues an opinion different than [his]." He contrasts this with an obvious reference to Mr. Peralta, the "salesman for democracy": "I know some of my colleagues, if you don't just bam bam, toe the line, they get a little upset. That's not important to me." Yet Mr. McGill's class is not, upon my observation, a hotbed of spirited debate. Several class periods were spent doing exercises out of the book in small groups, while two class periods were devoted to watching the popular movie, *The American President*, starring Michael Douglas. He takes a no-fluff, hard-nosed (dare I say, coach-like) attitude with his students, allowing them to know that he has no time for foolishness or flat-out stupidity: "And I think most of the kids know that I'm pretty laid back when it comes to a lot of things, but if you want to play the game, you know, the wrong way, you're going to lose" (Mr. McGill). He is large and intimidating in stature, so the students get the picture!

Still other teachers are more modest about their responsibilities. Mr. Kaupas, for example, has minimal requirements for his students to do well. He, by far, used less of the available class time (even with me observing) for discussions of Government than any of the other teachers. During my visits in March, a couple of classes did not "begin" until the college basketball game was over (a TV was wheeled into the room). Aside from that, no class would begin before Mr. Kaupas got into a lengthy discussion of popular subjects ranging from the success of the local high school or college sports teams to Pat Boone's heavy metal album that was released early in 1997. Topics were usually sparked by the morning comedy routines of syndicated radio shock-jocks Bob and Tom. Despite the claim that there was not enough time in the semester to cover everything, Mr. Kaupas made no attempt to overstate his objectives:

Well, you're kind of, in a way, I don't know if this is the best, but you're kind of a tour guide, you know. You got to be the guy who makes the decisions where you're going. You know I know it'd be nice to go to the kids, "well, what do you want to study?" A lot of times, you get no answer. So obviously, you're kind of guiding what you're going to study. But I kind of, what, really what I'd like to do when I get done, the thing I'd like to think I've done the most is kind of a facilitator in that, I mean, I obviously tell them what we want to talk about and bring up the topic, but then I just like to try to put our kids in a position where I don't simply lecture to them—although I do depend on that probably quite too much—but I like to get them to think and then come back and throw out questions to them and have them thinking and responding to what I'm telling them. So, if I can get them to think, that's what I want to try and get them to do.

While both Mr. Kaupas and Mr. McGill claim that they just "want the kids to think," they clearly have different approaches. By his own admission, Mr. Kaupas spends more time talking in class than does Mr. McGill, and the former is a significantly stronger proponent of the American political system. If teachers make a difference as to how students think and, subsequently, feel about the political system, we should expect that students in Mr. McGill's class would be significantly more critical than students in, say, Mr. Peralta's class (students who are ostensibly becoming "sold" on democracy) or Mr. Kaupas's class. Chapter 6 will examine whether or not this bears out with student survey data.

TEACHING ABOUT THE SUPREME COURT

What is most important for this study is to learn how each of these teachers approaches the Supreme Court. Students primarily learn about the Court in high school Government class through applied material about the Constitution, the Bill of Rights, and other civil liberties and rights. So even if the Court section gets excluded from the curriculum (as is often the case), the students are not, necessarily, deprived of information concerning the Court.

Having observed several classes during Court-related material, I began to notice that students seemed to be very interested in those topics—more so than in any of the other topics I witnessed. This trend held for virtually every class. I asked the teachers to estimate the students' interest in the Court as opposed to other topics, and their answers corroborated my observations.

Teachers were aware that I was most interested in the Court, and they seemed to be embarrassed about pushing that unit to the end of the semester.

Mr. Kaupas, for instance, tried to explain why he chose to cover the Court last: "You know, that's probably ironic. I would assume most kids by the time they get to us—you know I think we're guilty of it, too. You know, often times—I don't know if it's something like, subconsciously—often times, the Court's kind of put down toward the back. And we're kind of doing it here. Well, it's the last unit." Similarly, Mr. Caballero lamented the lack of time he had remaining in the semester to spend on the Court, noting "I've got four weeks left and I haven't really gone into real detail on the Supreme Court. . . . I mean, we haven't gotten into the chapters on the Supreme Court." So why is this? Why does the Court take a back seat to the other aspects of American Government?

The reasons are similar to those that members of the mainstream press might give if asked. The presidency is inherently interesting to students because they generally know who the president is and there have only been forty-two of them. The president is always in the news, and more people vote in the presidential elections than in any other. The Congress is the institution of the people. It is closest to the people (at the national level) and works along side the president to make policy for the country.

So the kids, they're probably most interested in a lot about the president, you know, because there is a personality and something they can relate to, whether it be the first family or Hillary or Chelsea or whatever, but the Court is probably the most removed part. . . . I think probably if anything we would get probably to the Court last because it's, we think, whether we're right or not, probably we're not, but we think, "well we've got to get to Congress." . . . How can you skip Congress? And how can you skip the electoral process of the president when it's such a multimedia event? And how can you skip the presidency? So it seems like the judiciary often gets . . . what time is left. (Mr. Kaupas)

He added, however:

And I don't know if that's necessarily right. I think it's just because it's the less observable or less obvious branch of the government, and as a result, you don't hear much about it unless they're making obviously some precedent-setting case or reversing a case. So I think . . . it's a good question. I think it just inadvertently gets left to the last. And usually we do, if I have time, it's usually a quick unit on the Court.

The operative word in the above passage, however, is "quick." Teachers were candid in saying that most often, the Court received merely a cursory review in class. So the initial answer to the question, "what are students learning about the Court in high school Government class?" is "little or nothing at all." But, as noted above, the Court gets covered in other sections of the course. Mr. Kaupas brings the Court into his discussion of the executive branch, stressing the importance of the president to the nomination of justices. As part of his sales pitch on the democratic way of life, Mr. Peralta explains to students that the Court has "been their friend" when it comes to guaranteeing their rights, saying that "the courts have done more than either the legislative or executive branches to protect and expand individual rights."

No teacher seemed to downplay the importance of the Supreme Court. There seems to be a recognition that since the Court is "the most removed" institution in the federal government, students are likely to overlook its impact. There is sometimes a special emphasis on the role of the Court that takes into account its political nature:

[I want students] to understand that this group of nine people can affect the interpretation of what we judge as the law of the land. . . . . We don't get real heavy duty into the federal court system, you know. Of all the time, we probably spend most, 90 or close per cent of the time totally on the Supreme Court [on] how people get their job, how do cases get to the Supreme Court. And again, just trying to get them to understand some of the process, but then the influence that the Supreme Court can have. And I also show them that based on who appoints whom in the Supreme Court, the fact that they can totally reinterpret the Constitution for potentially thirty, forty years and maybe even longer. So that's—I try to make the importance of the Court, in that unit, on the interpretation of the Constitution. (Mr. Kaupas)

Such information should translate into a more political interpretation of the Court by these students. A more political view of the Court, then, might allow these students to be more critical of it as a democratic institution. That is, the more "political" they understand the justices to be, the more mortal they appear to be. If students begin to see the Court and its members merely as additional players in the struggle for who gets what, when, and how, then they will be less likely to instill greater levels of confidence in them as opposed to the other national institutions (Congress and the presidency).

Some students, however, seem to be getting an equal dose of the Supreme Court institutionally as they are any other part of government. Mr. Hawk, as was his way, took a much more structured, packaged approach to teaching the Court. After thirty-six years, he was in a solid routine:

First of all, I have to define for them what the Supreme Court is—a lot of them think it's just a regular trial court, but just the judges have more power. So we approach it by saying, "OK, what kind of cases go to the Supreme Court?" We talk about its jurisdiction, its appellate or its original jurisdiction. And then, "how do you decide what cases?" And you break it down by the nature of the controversy and which party is involved. . . . Then we go through the procedure in the Court and we study some of the landmark cases. And then like right now the Supreme Court's coming out with decisions and things like that, we get that on the news, so that's something that kind of makes it more of a living thing. I think they get out of my class knowing more about the Supreme Court probably than they do about some other—I don' t want to say agencies—some other federal agencies. We cover the presidency pretty well and the Congress, but as far as a lot of—oh, what's the word I want?—regulatory agencies that deal with legalities and do law enforcement—they know more about the Court than they do those.

So while there are no claims that the Court is covered more than Congress or the presidency, it is covered more than, say, the Environmental Protection Agency or the FBI. But attitudes are less likely to be shaped by the quantity of class time devoted to the Court than by the way the Court is presented to students. The very fact that most teachers cover the Court primarily during the individual rights sections suggests that the Court is being portrayed as the guarantor of rights. If this is the case, it is reasonable to conclude that students will develop normatively positive attitudes about the Court, as it is difficult, in the abstract, to be *against* individual liberties (provided they are subscribing to the other tenants of democracy). We will examine, in chapter 6, the way in which a student's teacher does or does not influence various political attitudes.

USE OF THE TEXTBOOK

Students do not rely solely on their teacher for information. The textbook not only provides a source of information to the students but helps to structure the course and even, in some cases, provide information to the teachers. Chapter 5 contains an analysis of the most popular textbooks in the target state, but it is important to determine to what extent and in what capacity these books are used by the teachers.

Each teacher claimed that the textbook does not play an important role in his information gathering or structuring of the course. The story was similar: as young teachers, they relied on the textbook a lot for information and structure. As the years went on, they became familiar with the information in the texts and began to use them less. Now, even the youngest of the teachers finds that students respond better when they use the textbook less often: "You know, the kids kind of complain about, you know, 'we have to bring in the textbook, we have to pay for the textbook,' you know, I say, 'look, do you *really* want to read that textbook?' You know, 'sit down for 10 minutes and read that book and then tell me how much time you want to spend working with that thing.' And they get the point" (Mr. Caballero). Nearly all of the teachers claimed that they used the text as a "sourcebook" for students to supplement lectures and class discussions:

As far as some kind of chronology or anything, the book is pretty much—I don't really depend on the book to do anything in terms of the sequence or anything. . . . So, it's kind of a sourcebook, you know. I mean, we use it as a sourcebook, and I like to be able to have something for kids to hang their hat on and say, "okay, what we're doing now, even though it may be everything—we don't regurgitate the book, but now, this unit's focused on these two chapters." So, it's kind of a sourcebook for the kids. (Mr. Kaupas)

[P]ick up any high school text you want, and it's basically the same information. And so, as you well know, I give them outlines. And I tell them exactly what's going to be covered, and almost all of it is in the textbook, not all of it, there's some outside sources. But whether it's Magruder's or somebody else's, it doesn't make any difference. It's all there. But now, I don't assign specific assignments out of the textbook for the students.

I give—this is a resource. I say, "read this and maybe you'll understand better. If you're interested in anything, I would think you'd want to read this also in addition to listening to what is going on in class." But I don't assign any assignments at the end of the chapters. It's just strictly a resource, and a lot of students probably spend very little time— some students would tell you, "I never opened it." Because anything that's covered is going to be covered in class. (Mr. Peralta).

In fact, none of the teachers seemed terribly concerned about the upcoming textbook adoption.[8] They would have to live with the book they choose for the next six years, but still, none of them seemed to care which book was adopted. Mr. Hawk and Mr. McGill were both on the same adoption committee (they teach in the same school district) along with two parents. Mr. Hawk claimed that the parents "couldn't care less," but that Mr. McGill was fond of Magruder's. When I asked Mr. McGill what he liked about it, he replied, "Oh, they package it pretty nice. The pictures are up to date, color pictures, they use different color print. They highlight the important things. It's pretty thorough." That is hardly a ringing endorsement. Mr. Caballero similarly distanced himself from the book, saying "[It's] not very important. Not very important at all. Probably for each unit I teach, I'll have them do a core reading out of the book of maybe ten pages and they'll take a quiz over that. Everything else I pretty much bring in on my own. There are some units where I don't use the book at all."

But as we talked, many of the teachers' comments suggested a greater role for the texts:

Well, of course, the bulk of it comes from the book, but I present it in class, so they don't have to read the book to get it, see. And so I use the book, but I don't use it from a standpoint of assignments. Almost everything that's covered, like I say, is in the book, and they can use it if they think, "well, I need to—" They can use it as a resource. . . . And I tell them, I say, "I'm going to try to sell you on the democratic way of life. It's what I'm supposed to be doing. And you could leave this class with a very good understanding, and not be able to read a word. If you have a reading problem, don't worry about it. You don't have to read in this class. And I don't have time to teach you. But if you want to use the book, it's there to use. But that'll be up to you, see. But if you want to master this class, just be here every day, and listen and think about what I'm saying. Ask questions you don't understand and you'll get an A in this class. You never have to look at the textbook." But it is used because, you know—I got to the point where I don't feel like I need to read it anymore, I've read it so many times. (Mr. Peralta)[9]

Some teachers who originally downplayed the incorporation of the textbook into their classes even mentioned giving assignments out of the book:

And sometimes I don't give—I let them handle part of the book just on their own because the percentage that's going on to college are not going to have this sort of stuff spoon-fed to them, so I say, "this section's yours. You're taking care of this yourself." (Mr. Kaupas)

I do more worksheets and, you know, self-directed stuff than some other of my colleagues. They're basically lecturing. This class, you know, I mean half of them failed the first time around. And, you know, you don't want to call it busy work, but that's about the only way some of these kids are going to pass this class, if you give them something in black and white and say, "okay, do this, do this, do this. Here, use your book." (Mr. McGill)

I tell them what part I want them to read and then I just fill in a lot of stuff. And I have a lot of outside readings, too. (Mr. Hawk)

Yeah, I mean that gives me the basic structure and the basic concepts. . . . and then I take off from there, so I mean I use that and then really develop it more. . . . We can really go into some depth and read some outside stuff. I do bring in a lot of articles from the newspaper and from the Internet to kind of supplement the textbook. (Mr. Caballero)

So aside from Mr. Peralta (whose students, by his own admission, do not even have to be able to read), every teacher uses the book at least as a point of departure for studying American Government.

I got the impression that the book adoptions are primarily change for the sake of change. None of the teachers provided a very sound rationale for the switch, nor did anyone seem particularly excited about any book in particular. This might be because, as some of the teachers noted, there is not much difference among any of the standard American Government textbooks. Chapter 5 is devoted to an examination of these texts.

NOTES

1. They do not, however, vary with regard to gender. In fact, I was unable to locate any female social studies teachers in the area. Even those teachers who decided not to participate in the study were all male.

2. This teacher seemed to confuse technical points on occasion. For instance, when asked if he belonged to any professional organizations, he said that he was a member of "National Council of Social Studies, Indiana Council of Social Studies, American Academy of Political Science [and] Presidential Studies Quarterly." I am not aware of any American Academy of Political Science, so I assume he meant the American Political Science Association; and Presidential Studies Quarterly, though affiliated with the Center for the Study of the Presidency, is a journal, not a professional organization.

3. Mr. Caballero had not yet decided on a textbook for the next cycle.

4. A distinction needs to be made between "use" in the sense that this teacher wants his students to be active citizens, and the more empowering educational experience advocated by Freire (1968). While both seek to help students to navigate their political world, the former is concerned with concrete concepts such as understanding property and income taxes while the latter focuses on a more conceptual and theoretical understanding of the political system and the students' places within it.

5. "I got into education because I wanted to be a coach. And in those days they'd say, 'well, if you want to coach, you got to get a teaching license' " (Mr. Peralta).

6. It is true that promoting democracy does not necessarily mean promoting American democracy, but there were no indications either during the interview, nor during the twenty hours I spent in Mr. Peralta's classes, that he was distinguishing between an abstract idea of democracy and the reality of American democracy. Rather, he seemed a rather strong proponent of American democracy: "I respect the system. I think it's got to be the best place in the world to live."

7. All of the teachers were very conscious of what they said to their students regarding controversial issues. This is for the same reason that my project was looked upon suspiciously (and eventually banned) by at least one school: fear of parents' complaints. But the Catholic school teacher was particularly hesitant to make political statements in class. Having been warned that he may not, at any time, speak against the teachings of the Church, he became more cautious: "I don't even like to get close to it [sensitive political issues] because they [parents and students] will misinterpret what I say. So when I talk about something like that, a lot of times as they're taking notes, I'll just go ahead and write on the board 'Church says no birth control.' So now I know that that's documented in their notes" (Mr. Caballero). This greatly limits the parameters of discussion in class and consequently provides for a classroom that may be openly critical only when such criticism is in line with the Vatican.

8. As Table 4.1 shows, both of the districts (four teachers) who had made decisions on textbook adoption are changing books for the upcoming cycle.

9. While it is very disturbing that a teacher would outwardly admit that seniors in high school do not have to read to do well in his class, that is an entirely separate problem facing educators and education researchers. It is well beyond the scope of this book.

Chapter 5

American Government Textbooks

> Our children are learning about a government inspired by the revolutionary concept "We the People" from textbooks that downplay the role of the people.
> —Carroll *et al.* (1987)

While high school civics curricula have been found to have little or no effect on political socialization in general (Langton and Jennings 1968), there may be a stronger relationship between formal education and adult political orientations about issues that are less salient in the media. Formal political education necessarily fills a gap by relating to students that which they are unlikely to learn through other information sources. High school Government courses are (at least ostensibly) more concerned with "broad" issues of American democracy than are the media, as the former actively seek to educate a citizenry to meaningfully participate in the democratic process. These courses tend to portray the Court as the defender of the Constitution and guarantor of rights and liberties. Combined with the perceived distance that justices enjoy from politics and the Court's widely popular decisions concerning civil rights and liberties, this understanding of the Court's function makes it difficult for the public to blame the Court for their day-to-day frustrations and dissatisfaction.

THE ROLE OF TEXTBOOKS

Much of the content of high school Government classes comes from the adopted textbook. It is easy for academics to underestimate the importance of textbooks in a course. For professors, "textbooks" are generally only used in introductory-level classes. When academics do use textbooks, the lectures rarely mirror closely the information contained within; as researchers in the area under study, we are expected (and expect) to have an angle on the material that is not covered in the book. Such diversion from the information in the textbook is not as common in high schools.

Both the local school district and the state government are generally involved with developing a curriculum to be followed closely by classroom teachers. Despite the arguments against standardized testing, there is still a strong tendency to rely on state- or university-developed test scores when evaluating performance. To prepare students for these exams, teachers are made aware of what the students will be expected to know. In an eighteen-week course, there is little time for deviation from this curriculum.

Still, most of the teachers expressed an interest in moving beyond the texts in order to reach students. It is their sense that textbook material—no matter how colorful and flashy—bores students to tears. The real interest of politics, according to the teachers, must lie in the personal relevance students perceive in the material. But despite their intentions, teachers run into a myriad of problems when they attempt to supplement the textbook.

The most obvious barrier is time. Mr. Kaupas said that he "would love to spend about six weeks talking about voting behavior. The kids love that stuff, but we have to move on or we'll never get through the book by the end of the second term." Getting through the book is a chore. The four major American Government textbooks used in this state average over 750 pages each. That means that a teacher would have to assign over eight pages of reading each night in order to get through the book in an eighteen-week session. In reality, eight pages is the upper limit of reading that teachers typically assign for one evening, and they do not assign reading for every class period. Subsequently, there is not time to cover the "mandatory" reading, let alone delve more deeply into individual topics.

Teachers are often in the classroom twice as long as the average professor and are rewarded and promoted most heavily on their teaching, so it is unusual to find a high school teacher engaged in scholarly research on a regular basis. Social Studies teachers teach several subjects (most often History, Government, Economics, and/or Psychology and Sociology) and do not have the luxury of becoming "experts" in any one field or area. Add to this the responsibilities of coaching one or more school sports teams, and there is little time to develop a course that deviates noticeably from the text. Consequently, high school Government teachers rely heavily on the adopted textbook for both structure and content.[1]

COURT COVERAGE IN THE CLASSROOM VERSUS IN THE MEDIA

Citing one of his earlier studies, Richard Davis (1994) notes that "news coverage of the Court is slight compared to that devoted to the Congress or presidency" (21). Since people talk about what is in the news, it is unlikely that people are getting much information about the Court through interpersonal communication. Certainly popular culture has been obsessed with the criminal justice system, but it has yet to be determined whether or not general attitudes about the judiciary affect attitudes about the Supreme Court. In short, it is safe to surmise that we hear more about the Court during our formal political education than at any other time in our lives.

Time Devoted to the Court

But how much is that? Initially, we might guess that coverage of American politics in a high school American Government course would mirror that which is found in the media. On the other hand, we might consider that educators and textbook authors recognize their unique role in the American political system and seek to fill the gaps left by the media. *Schoolhouse Rock* notwithstanding, it would be difficult to learn how a bill becomes a law, for example, outside of school (unless we choose to undertake some research). Similarly, the Court's role in American politics is a subject largely limited to discussion in school. When the media does cover the Court, it is usually either to report a decision, a nomination, or a retirement. Elliot Slotnick and Jennifer Segal (1998) explain that "this emphasis on the docket reflects the insulated nature of the Court, its distance from the rest of the political world, and the difficulty that reporters have in gaining access to the inner workings of Supreme Court processes and the relationship among its members" (167). "Larger" questions about the Court's role in American democracy are not news items and are generally absent from the media.

High school American Government courses tend to be heavily concerned with the Constitution, freedom and equality, and civil rights and liberties. Since the Supreme Court has made landmark decisions on these concepts and issues, its decisions are likely to be incorporated throughout the book, not just in the chapter on the judiciary. Anticipating that textbook authors are, indeed, attempting to fill gaps with regard to the Court and focusing on constitutional issues, we might anticipate that the Court is presented as much as, or more than, Congress or the presidency in high school American Government textbooks.

Impact and the Justices

Two qualitative hypotheses are also worthy of consideration. First, the Court's power to make or impact public policy is underappreciated in the mass public. As Davis (1994) acknowledges, this is largely due to intentional and active efforts by the Court to preserve an image of unanimity, independence from the other branches, distance from the political process and the public, and immunity from political pressure (5-7). These tactics preserve the Court's apolitical image and allow it to avoid being the target of the bulk of public dissatisfaction. Court justices must be delighted to have their politicalness underestimated, since the reality would likely compromise the Court's image of "impartial defender of the Constitution," and thereby threaten to undermine its legitimacy. But again, the Court's political power is not news, which leaves yet another gap to be filled by educators. So with respect to the *impact* of Court decisions, we should expect high school American Government textbooks to stress the importance of the Supreme Court in shaping public policy.

Part of Davis's (1994) argument about the Court's image-making efforts is that justices help to retain the legitimacy of the institution by perpetuating the perception that they are (collectively and individually) above politics. However, by introducing the Court during chapters on civil rights and liberties, for example, textbook authors imply an undeniably political side to the Court. Further, it is the responsibility of the American Government course to fully introduce students to the Court and its members, including discussion of the political process of nomination and confirmation. This is not the case with the press. As ABC News' Tim O'Brien told Slotnick and Segal (1998), "by and large we don't cover the people—we cover what they do" (167). It would be impossible for textbook authors to ignore the political nature of the Court's members as the press often does. Thus, Supreme Court justices are likely acknowledged as political beings in high school American Government textbooks.

Realization of these three hypotheses means that American Government textbooks cover the Court both quantitatively more and qualitatively differently than the mainstream media do. If this is so, there will be reason to suspect a greater role of the American Government textbook in the formation of attitudes about the Court, as opposed to other political attitudes.

DATA AND METHOD

Table 1.2 listed the four textbooks that are used in 95 per cent of the target state's school districts. I obtained the 1996 edition of each book directly from the publishers and examined them for content.[2]

FINDINGS

If the school is the primary source of information during adolescence, then the Government class should be the primary source of information about American politics for high school students. It is true, however, that students are likely to obtain knowledge about politics in ways they would not about, say, mathematics or chemistry. The mainstream media outlets are full of information about American politics, and parents and peers are more likely to informally relay sentiments about social and political issues than about any other school subject. Still, five hours per week in class plus homework time afford students the opportunity to think most deeply (or at least at length) about their political world. But how much of that time is spent thinking about the judiciary? How much do they learn about the Supreme Court?

Table 5.1 reveals that the four textbooks under consideration spent an average of 13 per cent of the book on Congress, 11 per cent on the presidency, and

15 per cent on the Supreme Court. In terms of the number of pages devoted to political institutions (around 288 on average), 33 per cent of those pages were devoted to Congress, 28 per cent were spent on the presidency, and 39 per cent focued on the judiciary (primarily the Supreme Court). These findings lend considerable support to the quantitative hypothesis that textbooks spend more time on the Court than on either of the other two branches, and are graphically depicted in Figure 5.1.[3]

Part of the reason the Court receives more coverage than the other two branches is the importance of Court rulings to policy issues—particularly regarding civil rights and liberties. The four texts report an average of 172 cases.[4] Such emphasis on the Court's role in policymaking paints a political image of the Court that is not generally found to exist among the mass public. But it may be the presentation of the Court beyond the cases that has the most effect on the way we learn about it.

We cannot make any determination about the impact on students of information presented in Government textbooks simply by acknowledging that more time is spent on the judiciary than on the other branches. It is important to note what kind of attention the textbook authors pay to the Court. Court coverage can generally be broken down into four interrelated areas: the Court's *function* in American democracy, the *process* by which the Court arrives at decisions, the *impact* Court rulings have on public policy, and the way *justices* are depicted.

Function and Process

The role of political institutions is often romanticized in a historical, near mythic depiction of the founders' intentions. Consider this description of the Supreme Court building used to introduce students to the Court:

The eagle, the flag, Uncle Sam—you almost certainly recognize these symbols. They are widely used to represent the United States. You probably also know the symbol for justice—the blindfolded woman holding a balanced scale. She represents what is perhaps the nation's highest goal: equal justice for all. Indeed, those words are chiseled into the marble above the entrance of the Supreme Court building in Washington, D.C. (McClenaghan 1996, 471).

And from Remy (1996), the caption below picture of the Supreme Court building reads:

The frieze above the entrance to the Supreme Court building in Washington, D.C., reminds all who enter that the Court's primary goal is the safeguarding of justice and equality as guaranteed in the United States Constitution (571).

Function. These descriptions set the stage for a discussion of the Supreme Court rooted deeply in the importance of that institution for the preservation of American democracy. The early pages of the chapter on the Court tend to cen-

Table 5.1
Number of Textbook Pages Devoted to Each Branch of Government

Textbook	Total Pages	Pages on Institutions	Congress	Presidency	Supreme Court
Hardy	805	355 (44%)	121 (15%) **34% of inst. pages**	93 (12%) **26% of inst. pages**	141 (18%) **40% of inst. pages**
McClenaghan	685	323 (47%)	106 (15%) **33% of inst. pages**	88 (13%) **27% of inst. pages**	129 (19%) **40% of inst. pages**
Remy	884	244 (28%)	70 (8%) **29% of inst. pages**	82 (9%) **34% if inst. pages**	92 (10%) **38% of inst. pages**
Turner, Switzer and Redden	706	228 (32%)	84 (12%) **37% of inst. pages**	55 (8%) **24 % of inst. pages**	89 (13%) **39% of inst. pages**

Source: Hardy (1996); McClenaghan (1996); Remy (1996); and Turner, Switzer, and Redden (1996).

Note: Cell numbers are raw number of pages. The number in parentheses is the percentage of total pages, while the bold number below in the institutions' cells represents the percentage of pages on institutions consumed by each branch of government. Percentages are rounded.

Figure 5.1
American Government Textbooks: Pages Devoted to Each Branch of Government

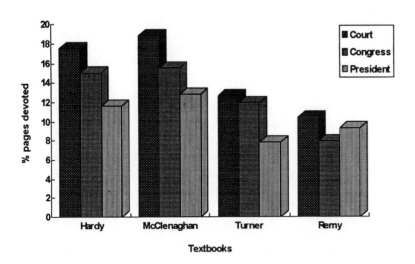

Source: Hardy (1996); McClenaghan (1996); Remy (1996); Turner, Switzer, and Redden (1996).

Note: Y-axis numbers represent the percentage of total pages in the book devoted to each branch of the federal government.

ter around the unique position the Court holds. The first paragraph about the Supreme Court in Turner, Switzer, and Redden (1996) outlines the Court's *function* in America: "The Supreme Court of the United States is the final authority in all questions arising under the Constitution, federal laws, and national treaties. It is the legal center of American life, and its decisions have a strong impact on social, economic, and political forces in our society" (477). Such strong language certainly does not overstate the role of the Court in the American system, but it emphasizes the tendency most people have to overlook this role. The authors want to be sure that the reader understands the current and historical importance of the Court, regardless of how seldom the Court appears in the news.

Most important, however, is the recognition that the Court is presented as the "final authority in all questions arising under the Constitution." If there is one concept in American society that has a virtually unchallenged place among the core of American values, it is that of a virtuous Constitution. Very few people criticize the Constitution publicly; even when we argue about issues of constitutional law, it usually takes place within the confines of the language of the original document, assuming its righteousness (West 1993). If the Court is portrayed as the institution with "final authority" over Constitutional issues— "the final interpreter of the Constitution" (Hardy 1996, 468)—it necessarily becomes more fundamental to democracy than the other branches.

Indeed, the Court's near-anointed status is reinforced by the assertion that justices are not subject to the same pressures (and potential evils) as "politicians":

Members of the Court are intentionally insulated from public and political pressure so that their decisions will be as rational as humanly possible. The job of a justice is not to make law but rather to interpret and apply laws that others have made. (Turner, Switzer, and Redden 1996, 485)

Legal realists would argue this point, but it is presented to students as fact. In effect, the above passage serves to dissuade students from considering justices in the same light as members of Congress or the president, the "others" to whom the authors refer. The justices are set apart from the "others" and "insulated" against their pressure. So however one feels about Congress and the president, one does not necessarily need to feel the same way about Supreme Court justices because they have a different function: "to interpret" and "apply," not "make" law.

Process. The above passage also hints at another difference between the Court and other political institutions: that of *process.* By the time students reach their senior year of high school, they are aware that politicians are pressured by various sources on a daily basis. Whether or not a student can explain the presence and influence of interest groups, party leaders, other elected officials, and the mass public, he or she would not question their existence. The students are told, however, that the process by which Supreme Court justices make decisions is more "rational," since they are "insulated" from such pressure. In fact, during their decision-making time, they are insulated from everything and everyone:

Justices of the Supreme Court hear oral arguments concerning all cases in a courtroom open to the public. However, much of their work is accomplished in judicial conference rooms and in their private offices. (Turner, Switzer and Redden 1996, 483)

On Wednesdays and Fridays throughout a term, the justices meet in conference. There, in closest secrecy, they consider the cases in which they have heard oral arguments. (McClenaghan 1996, 476)

Each Friday morning during the term is a private conference day when the justices meet to discuss petitions and cases they have heard and vote on final decisions. Only the justices are present, and no records are kept of the discussion within the conference.

At least six of the nine justices must be present to decide a case. The chief justice begins discussion with a summary of the facts and an analysis of the law in each case. Next, the associate justices, in order of seniority, all present their views. (Turner, Switzer, and Redden 1996, 483)

On Fridays the justices meet in conference to discuss the cases they have heard. The nine justices come into the conference room and, by tradition, each shakes hands with the other eight. Everyone else leaves. Then one of the most secret meetings in Washington, D.C., begins. (Remy 1996, 572)

In the era of C-SPAN and C-SPAN II, such a distinctive decision-making environment certainly separates the justices from their counterparts in Congress and the executive branch. A very structured process is presented, showing consideration of seniority and the leadership of the chief justice. But most notable is the constant emphasis on secrecy. If part of the Court's legitimacy is perpetuated by its mystery, high school Government books are contributing greatly to the Court's objective. Students must ask themselves, "Why must this branch operate in such secrecy when the other two branches are so visible?" The suggested answer implies the importance of the Court's work and the resulting necessity for the Court to be removed from the evils of the public.

So while textbooks cover quantitatively more than the media do, the substance of the Court's coverage thus far does not appear to differ from the way the Court is presented in the media.

Judicial Impact and the Justices

Recall that there are two hypothesized qualitative characteristics that relate specifically to the content of Government textbooks with regard to the Court. The first is that textbook authors focus on the importance of the Court's rulings for public policy, while the second is that justices would be acknowledged as political beings.

Judicial Impact. Perhaps the most important aspect of the Court's activities involves the lasting effect it can have on public policy. Public frustration with the American political system is generally directed toward the president or Congress, since it is members of these institutions who are directly elected by the people. Consequently, Supreme Court justices are not often considered to be "politicians," despite their ability to make or change public policy. Students learn that the Supreme Court, "through its interpretation of the law and the Constitution . . . has played a part in making public policy throughout our history [and that] the Court's interpretations of laws and the Constitution have profound effect on public policy" (Turner, Switzer, and Redden 1996, 485, 486). But only Remy (1996) directly addresses the distinctly political side to the Court, noting that "[t]he Supreme Court is both a political and legal institution. It is a legal institution because it is ultimately responsible for settling disputes and interpreting the meaning of laws. The Court is a political institution because when it applies the law to specific disputes it often determines what national policy will be" (564). There is a subtle, yet important distinction between the above passage by Remy and the previous quote from Turner, Switzer, and Redden. An apolitical view of the Court would still allow for "play[ing] a part in making public policy" and "hav[ing] a profound effect on public policy." Remy's language specifically spells out that the Court has the potential to do a job that the Constitution apparently reserves for the other two branches. Only this kind of recognition allows students to fully comprehend that the Court can be (and often is) political beyond the narrow constructs of judicial interpretation.

This sends a mixed message to the student. That is, most books (and even most of Remy's book) do not focus on the political nature of the Court's actions per se, but, as noted above, a large amount of discussion about the Court comes in chapters about civil rights and liberties—two political concepts. Still, each book spends considerable time discussing the Court's role in shaping public policy (even if the discussion is not grounded in the political nature of such actions), which lends support to the contention that the textbooks stress the importance of the Court's policymaking role.

The Justices. Davis (1994) asserts that media coverage of the Court is particularly lacking in personal stories (apart from the selection and appointment process) and heavy on reporting of salient cases.[5] But, as Table 5.1 suggests, Court coverage in Government textbooks is quite different than it is in the media.

Most media reports about the Court focus on decisions, and very few involve the justices individually, let alone personally (Davis 1994). As Slotnick and Segal (1998) report:

Our analysis of the 1989 and 1994 Court terms reveals quite clearly that television network news coverage of the Court is somewhat unbalanced in its focus on the Court. For example, emphasis is placed on the Court's docket work, to the relative exclusion of any other Court-related activities and the justices themselves; the exception to this, as both terms illustrate, is the resignation and appointment of justices, which attracts relatively substantial coverage when it occurs. (187)

In fact, the justices wish to maintain an image that is above individuality, above the political, and, in most cases, beyond the personal. Politics is a personal phenomenon, and the screen of the Court's collective (if not always unified) image dissuades the impression that politics is at work.

The justices are presented a bit differently to students. As might be expected, some of the text centers on the responsibilities of the justices: "The duties of the justices include selecting which cases to hear, deciding those cases, and writing legal opinions about their decisions. . . . The most important work of the Court involves the justices in three major tasks. These are selecting which cases to hear from among the thousand that come before them, deciding the cases, and explaining the reasoning behind the decisions" (Turner, Switzer, and Redden 1996, 479). But treatment of the justices in American Government textbooks tends to move past job descriptions. Pictures of the justices appear in all four books; remarks appearing in the captions of Turner, Switzer, and Redden (1996) are listed in Table 5.2. Unlike the coverage of the Court in the mainstream press, these authors use the few sentences they have about the justices individually to note, in several cases, preferred ideology or reputation.

It can be argued that the information contained in Table 5.2 consists of that which is "understood" or "known" in the general public about each of these justices, even if the vast majority of Americans can not name even a single justice (reported in Epstein *et al.* 1994, 702). If we know what president nominated a justice, we can make an educated guess at that justice's ideology. But this cognitive process does not hold for students for two interrelated reasons: (1) more than likely, this American Government course is the first place they have even heard the name of a currently sitting justice; and (2) if they do know of a justice, they are unlikely to remember his or her appointment and subsequent confirmation hearings. These points are important because in order to link a justice with a president to determine the former's ideology, one must know the justice, know the appointing president, and know the president's ideology (at least roughly). Turner, Switzer, and Redden (1996), despite devoting only a couple of sentences to individual justices, are certain to alert the reader to the fact that justices are ideological (political) beings—something the mainstream media leave behind after the confirmation hearings.

It is precisely those hearings when justices are likely to get most of the media attention they will receive in their careers (with retirement or death running a close second). The textbooks reinforce the inescapably political nature of the process:

The same factors that influence the President in choosing lower court judges are at work in the President's choice of a nominee to the Supreme Court. These factors, remember, include a candidate's political party, personal background, and experience. Presidents also choose candidates whose political philosophies are similar to their own. That is, conservative presidents seek out conservatives and liberal presidents try to place liberals on the bench. (Turner, Switzer, and Redden 1996, 479)

A portrait is painted of a political person nominating another political person (since party and political philosophy are taken into account), through a political process (confirmation by the senate), for an ostensibly nonpolitical position. This is enough to cause even the most casual student of American Government (which most high school students are) to have some suspicions about the apolitical role of the Court. And textbooks are not shy about noting that justices disagree on political issues, even if the disagreements are framed in terms of constitutional interpretation:

[J]ustices often disagree sharply about how to interpret the law. . . . In recent years, the Court has split on a number of crucial issues such as the death penalty and abortion. (Turner, Switzer, and Redden 1996, 483)

Those disagreements and ultimate decisions, the authors note, have real consequences for American Government.

Table 5.2
Remarks in Photo Captions about Sitting Justices

Justice	_Page_	_Quote_
Breyer	484	"Stephen Breyer became an associate justice of the Supreme Court in 1994. Before serving on the Su preme Court, Breyer had served as appellate Court judge."
Ginsberg	478	"President Clinton appointed Ruth Bader Ginzberg *[sic]*, a judge on the United States Court of Appeals, to the Supreme Court in 1993. She is the second woman to serve on the Court."
Kennedy	477	"Anthony Kennedy, known for his **conservative views** on constitu tional issues, was appointed a Su preme Court associate Justice in 1987."
O'Connor	481	"Profile: The First Woman on the Supreme Court" An entire page is devoted to Sandra Day O'Connor. Some comments include: "On the bench, Associate Justice O'Connor is known as a careful legal thinker with a **respect for legal precedent**. She has **generally supported judicial restraint**. . . . However, O'Connor has not favored judicial restraint in every case, nor has she voted exclusively with the majority."
Rehnquist	479	"William Rehnquist is the current chief justice of the Supreme Court. Appointed to the post in 1986, Rehnquist had earlier served as an associate justice for 14 years."
Scalia	483	"Antonin Scalia is an associate justice of the Su preme Court. He was named to the post in 1986."
Souter	482	"David Souter became an associate justice of the Supreme Court in 1990. On Supreme Court cases, Souter has taken **moderate positions**."
Stevens	485	"Associate Justice John Paul Stevens is known for his **moderate decisions**."

Table 5.2 (continued)

Justice	*page*	*Quote*
Thomas	485	"Associate Justice Clarence Thomas has **moderate to conservative** viewpoints."

Source: Turner, Switzer, and Redden (1996).

Note: Emphasis is added. All quotes are taken from the captions associated with each justice's picture. Justice O'Connor was the subject of an entire page "box" profile; remarks for her are excerpts.

But even as the justices are described as political beings, textbook authors make an effort to point out that these are not ordinary politicians. Remy writes: "To maintain their objectivity on the bench, justices are careful not to become involved in outside activities that might prevent them from dealing fairly with one side or the other on a case. If justices have any personal or business connection with either of the parties in a case, they usually disqualify themselves from participating in that case" (1996, 555). Still, students are urged to consider the justices' humanity: "Supreme Court justices, like other political figures, are people with active interests in important issues" (Remy 1996, 575). Hardy notes that

[b]ecause Supreme Court justices are appointed for life terms, many Americans have the impression that justices are isolated from the stresses of politics. They do escape much of the pressure that elected officials face. . . .

Supreme Court justices nevertheless face public pressure. They are supposed to remain independent, unbiased protectors of the Constitution. Yet, they are also human beings who read newspapers, watch television, receive mail, and converse with friends. Moreover, they can never totally ignore public opinion. (1996, 481)

By the end of the book (course), all this discussion results in a mixed message about Supreme Court justices: they are inherently political beings, but they are not supposed to be, so they do everything they can to isolate themselves from the public and political pressure to maintain their independence.

DISCUSSION

It has been apparent for some time that adults do not know much about the Supreme Court. The findings in this chapter suggest that the Court is not neglected in high school Government textbooks as it is in the media, but it is covered more often and often as a political, as well as a legal, institution. At the same time, however, the Court is presented as a privileged branch, designed to defend the virtuous Constitution, presumably against infringement by popularly elected officials. Set apart from the "political" branches, the Court has enjoyed greater public confidence due to this perception of its role, perpetuated in the mainstream media, as well as through the schools.

Because of the attention paid to the political aspects of the Court, however, high school students may, indeed, learn about the Court as a political institution. If this is so, that information is apparently lost throughout the course of one's adulthood, so that Congress and the presidency are evaluated more critically. Comparatively low media coverage creates an "out of sight, out of mind" situation where people think about (and fault) the "political" branches more often than they do the Court.

Alternately, students' political or social predispositions (acquired through other agents of socialization) may override the political information about the Court received during formal education. Tom Tyler (1990) found that people obey laws (have respect for the legal system) largely because of their normative social values (178). That is, people are taught early on what is "right and proper," and their attitudes and behaviors follow from those preconceptions. If students bring to their reading of the textbooks attitudes about the proper role of legal authority in general, or the American justice system more specifically, we must consider that those attitudes color the students' reading of their American Government textbooks.

A fuller, more contextual analysis of the American high school student is needed to more accurately determine the base of the Court's support.

NOTES

1. Textbook publishers are increasingly aware of the time constraints placed on teachers, so they have adapted their books accordingly: multimedia packets are widely available to supplement the text, offering video tapes and exercises to illustrate the information provided in the book. This further eliminates the need for teachers to take it upon themselves to seek out additional information to supplement the textbook.

2. Most content analysis applies standardized measurement to metrically defined units in order to characterize and compare documents (Manning and Cullum-Swan 1994, 464; see also Weber 1990). I am not concerned with comparisons among the four texts; rather, I wish simply to note trends and tendencies regarding treatment of the Supreme Court.

3. Of course, just because material is in the textbook does not mean that it will be covered in the course. As noted above, there is rarely time to cover all the material in a textbook during an eighteen week course.

4. The range, however, is notable. McClenaghan reports 299 cases, where Turner, Switzer, and Redden only report 64. Remy and Hardy include 129 and 196 cases respectively.

5. I use the word "heavy" in a relative sense. Davis is not claiming that there is heavy coverage of Court decisions, rather that of the news stories about the Court, most of them focus on the reporting of cases. We might contrast this with the personal stories we see about the president (golfing, vacationing, jogging, etc.) and members of Congress (often getting into trouble).

Chapter 6

Teachers Matter

A review of the socialization literature in chapter 2 revealed that research in this area tapered off largely because scholars had shown formal political education to be largely unrelated to many adult political attitudes. Further, researchers began to understand that political learning does not generally end in childhood but continues on well into one's adult life. But attitudes that are less likely to be challenged later in life are more likely to reflect those formed during early or adolescent socialization.

Moving toward an empirical confirmation of this hypothesis, it is important to determine what students learn about the Supreme Court in their mandatory American Government or Civics courses in high school, and how that affects diffuse support for the Court. Based on the theoretical framework stated above, I now move to an examination of high school students' attitudes about the Supreme Court and other American political institutions, to determine whether or not differences exist between students with different teachers. If a student's teacher is an important factor in determining support for or opposition to the Supreme Court, there will be sufficient reason to continue exploration of how these differences might substantively affect that level of support.

DATA AND METHOD

The survey (see the Appendix) was self-administered and taken in class for seven of the classes and at home for three of the classes (because of the principal's requirements[1]). The questionnaire covers many aspects of a student's political development, including media exposure, ideology and party identification, attitudes about American political institutions and political issues, demographic characteristics, and specific questions about the Supreme Court. Students were asked to indicate their preferences on Likert scales, as well as give written answers to open-ended questions. What follows is an overview of student responses to questions regarding support for the Court and some preliminary findings about relationships among some of these variables.

DIFFERENCES BETWEEN ADULTS AND STUDENTS

The student sample is considerably whiter than that of the general public, but it is otherwise quite similar.[2] The students are a bit more conservative and more Republican than American adults nationwide, but that slight difference is most likely accountable to geography (the state is in the midwest).

As shown in Figure 6.1, students have more confidence in each institution than do the adults. Students have the greatest level of confidence in the military, closely followed by confidence in the Supreme Court. While students' confidence in the three branches of government are, in the aggregate, a bit higher than the mass public, the general trend of considerably more support for the Court than the other branches holds. This is telling. It points to the cynicism that has largely engulfed the American public with regard to the political world. Whether it is a life-cycle effect, resulting from more experience with American politics, or a cohort effect, stemming largely from memories of Watergate (which none of the students are old enough to remember), the students are more confident in the people running each of the institutions. Like the adults in 1998, students have the greatest amount of confidence in the military, followed closely by the Supreme Court.

STUDENT ATTITUDES

The high school students in this study were asked to identify their positions on Gregory Caldeira and John Gibson's (1992) five questions designed to tap diffuse support for the Court, and the results appear in the first part of Table 6.1.[3] As expected, students' attitudes on each of these issues show that they are reluctant to endorse legal or constitutional action that would limit the power of the Court or do away with the Court altogether. While this may not be particularly surprising, it is notable that this is the case even though students are not as likely to agree with the Court on some of their salient rulings, as is evidenced by the second part of Table 6.1. While students are in favor of the Court's rulings on capital punishment and, to a lesser extent, mandatory prayer in public school, their attitudes are evenly split with regard to abortion. So it appears that, in the aggregate, students are likely to have a high level of diffuse support for the Court, irrespective of their level of specific support for Court decisions.

Table 6.1
Attitudes about the Supreme Court (Students)

	Strongly Agree/ Agree	Strongly Disagree/ Disagree	Not Sure	Diffuse Factor	Specific Factor
"The power of the Supreme Court to declare acts of Congress unconstitutional should be eliminated."	12 (6.4%)	128 (68.4%)	47 (25.1%)	.748	-.187
"If the Supreme Court continually makes decisions that people disagree with, it might be better to do away with the Court altogether."	14 (7.5%)	135 (72.2%)	38 (20.3%)	.695	.219
"It would not make much difference to me if the United States Constitution were rewritten so as to reduce the powers of the Supreme Court."	22 (11.8%)	122 (65.2%)	43 (23.0%)	.740	-.189
"The power of the Supreme Court to decide certain types of controversial issues should be limited by the Congress."	49 (26.1%)	80 (42.6%)	59 (31.4%)	.656	-.017

Table 6.1 (continued)

	Strongly Agree/ Agree	Strongly Disagree/ Disagree	Not Sure	Diffuse Factor	Specific Factor
"People should be willing to do everything they can to make sure that any proposal to abolish the Supreme Court is defeated."	95 (50.8%)	27 (14.4%)	65 (34.8%)	**-.685**	.081
"The United States Supreme Court was correct in ruling that a woman has the constitutional right to decide whether or not to carry a pregnancy to full term."	83 (44.4%)	83 (44.4%)	21 (11.2%)	.115	**.771**
"The United States Supreme Court was correct in ruling that no state or local government may require the reading of the Lord's Prayer or Bible verses in public schools."	115 (61.2%)	49 (26.1%)	23 (12.2%)	-.212	**.691**

	Strongly Agree/ Agree	Strongly Disagree/ Disagree	Not Sure	Diffuse Factor	Specific Factor
"The United States Supreme Court was correct in ruling that the death penalty for people convicted of murder is not, under most circumstances, cruel and unusual punishment."	139 (74.3%)	33 (17.6%)	15 (8.0%)	-.069	**.647**

Note: Column figures are raw numbers of student respondents. Percentages appear in parentheses. Responses were indicated on a five-point Likert scale that has only been collapsed for presentation purposes in this table. All variables have been coded so that *higher values indicate greater levels of agreement* with the statements. Factor solutions are varimax rotated.

Figure 6.1
Adults' and Students' Confidence in American Political Institutions

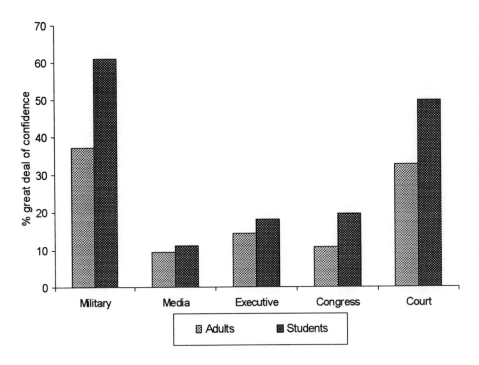

Source: Davis and Smith (1998).

A principal components analysis confirms the hypothesis that attitudes about specific Court decisions are distinct from general feelings of goodwill toward the Court as an institution. Placing all of the items in a single analysis, two factors are extracted that clearly indicate this distinction. These items will be indexed and used in their component form for the remainder of this analysis.[4]

Impressions of the Supreme Court

Students were asked to name one institution that they felt best protects their rights. No options were provided, and answers ranged from the FBI and CIA to the ACLU, and from the fire department to the FAA. The Supreme Court, however, was listed by over half of the students who gave answers and nearly 40 per cent of all students surveyed. In contrast, Congress was mentioned by 8 per cent of the students and the president by merely 2 per cent. This is illustrative of the way that students learn about the Court—in the context of protecting and preserving civil rights and liberties.

When specifically asked to write what they thought to be the role of the Court, nearly 20 per cent had no answer to offer. Of the students that did answer, however, 18 per cent said that the Court is supposed to "protect us," "keep the peace," or "promote justice." The plurality (26 per cent) listed "deciding large/constitutional issues" as the primary role of the Court. Still another 14 per cent said that they believe the Supreme Court is supposed to "defend the constitution" or "protect constitutional rights." Other notable responses were "interpret the laws" (the "textbook" answer), "check government," and "work for the people's best interests." Disturbingly, some students indicated that the Court was supposed to "enforce laws," while others claimed that it should "make laws."

Curious about how interested students are about the Court, I asked them to rank their interest in the three branches of the federal government. Students, in the aggregate, are most interested in the president and least interested in the Supreme Court. In fact, 56 per cent of students ranked the Court third of the three branches, while only 12 per cent were most interested in it. Of all the students, 73 per cent of the students were most interested in the president. This is consistent with the personal nature of American politics; the institution to which it is most easy to attach a face commands the most interest, while that which is most difficult to personify is the least interesting to students.

That lack of personification benefits the Court insofar as students are likely to consider justices to be politicians. Sixty-seven per cent of the students believed that justices are not politicians. When asked why not, most students reported that "they are not elected." Other responses included: "they just don't fit the [model] of a politician," "they follow the rules, not their political views," and "they are immune from politics."[5] Of the students who did see justices as politicians, the plurality claimed that it was because justices are "heavily involved in politics" or "are appointed by politicians." Sadly, however, 12 per cent of students who thought justices are politicians believed so because "they are elected."

Media Exposure and Interpersonal Communication

Level of media exposure should not be particularly relevant to attitudes about the Court since mainstream media outlets so seldom cover the Court, especially when compared with the other two branches of government. To test that notion, media exposure to two primary outlets was measured: print media (newspaper and news magazines) and broadcast media (network and local television news and radio).[6] As Table 6.2 shows, students claim to watch local news and read a newspaper (primarily a local newspaper, as indicated by the open-ended responses that followed this item on the questionnaire) more frequently than they participate in any of the other activities. As expected, the items load nicely onto two factors.

It is also important to determine to what extent students may or may not be influenced by other agents of socialization—namely, the family and peer group.

Table 6.2
Level of Media Exposure (Students)

	5-7 Times Per Week	2-4 Times Per Week	About Once a Week	Never	Mean	Print Factor	Broadcast Factor
Read a daily newspaper	77 (40.7%)	63 (33.3%)	40 (21.2%)	9 (4.8%)	3.10	.125	**.748**
Read news magazines	6 (3.2%)	26 (13.8%)	70 (37.2%)	86 (45.7%)	1.74	.063	**.802**
Watch network news	37 (19.7%)	63 (33.5%)	54 (28.7%)	34 (18.1%)	2.55	**.691**	.229
Watch local news	47 (24.9%)	84 (44.4%)	48 (25.4%)	10 (5.3%)	2.89	**.763**	.056
Listen to talk radio	37 (19.8%)	32 (17.1%)	32 (17.1%)	86 (46.0%)	2.11	**.687**	.021

Note: Students were asked to "please indicate how often [they] participate in the activity." Column figures are raw number of responses. Percentages appear in parentheses. Responses were indicated on a four-point Likert scale. All variables have been recoded so that *higher values indicate greater frequency of the activity*. Factor solutions are varimax rotated.

According to the teachers, students are getting little or no informal political information, although some students receive more than others:

I've got some students in here that I think their families are really pretty politically astute..... I've got some kids where their parents are politically active in the party locally and some even beyond that, statewide, some even have been, one had been to a national convention. But I think for the most part, really, the larger percentage, politics is something that just kind of goes on but it's not part of their lives. . . . So I don't know, I think for some kids, this is the only place. (Mr. Kaupas)

A very small percentage of them come in being regular news watchers and newspaper readers. Probably not more than 10 to 15, maybe 20 per cent. Many of them irregularly follow politics. So they'll come in and they'll have an idea—they'll ask me about something that they saw on TV, but they don't have much knowledge about it, but they just happened to be watching the news that night. . . . So they come in with varying amounts, but every year I've got one or two kids who are really news junkies and are really tuned in and I've always got people that have no absolutely no clue, absolutely no clue. (Mr. Caballero)

The better students, they're pretty well informed. I'm kind of shocked at the students who have no interest in—we just went through an election. And there were kids who couldn't even tell me who was running for president. There were kids who didn't know who Bob Dole was. You know to me, of course, I watch the news so I see—but it seems that there's very little they bring, except the better students who comes from a family who is actively involved in politics and have a good educational background. (Mr. Hawk)

Right now I don't think they spend much time at all thinking about politics . . . They're more concerned about who went to the prom with who, who got what for graduation, whose party was a blowout, whose was a drag (laughs). (Mr. McGill)

To gauge how often students engaged in discussion about politics with their families and peers, respondents were asked to indicate how often they talked about the president, Congress, the Supreme Court, or political issues with both their parents and their friends. The results appear in Table 6.3.

Students report talking most frequently about the president. This is not surprising since the president is the most visible political actor in the country and generates the greatest amount of media attention. Similarly, political issues are the second most frequently discussed political topic among high school seniors in this sample. At an age where social concerns are quickly becoming more and more personally relevant, we should expect that topics like abortion, legalization of marijuana, contraception distribution in the schools, and other timely issues would generate substantial attention from teens. Students are less likely to talk about the Supreme Court with either parents or friends than they are to talk about either of the other two branches of government. A principal components analysis of all eight items produced two distinct, yet interrelated factors: talking to parents about politics and talking to friends about politics.[7] This

Table 6.3
Interpersonal Communications about Politics (Students)

	Regularly	Sometimes	Hardly Ever	Never	Mean	Parents Factor	Friends Factor
How often do you talk to your parents about:							
The president	19 (10.1%)	98 (51.9%)	49 (25.9%)	23 (12.2%)	2.60	**.847**	.165
Political issues	20 (10.6%)	69 (36.5%)	70 (37.0%)	30 (15.9%)	2.42	**.875**	.163
Congress	4 (2.1%)	24 (12.7%)	77 (40.7%)	84 (44.4%)	1.72	**.769**	.399
The Supreme Court	2 (1.1%)	18 (9.6%)	73 (38.8%)	95 (50.5%)	1.61	**.681**	.424
How often do you talk to your friends about:							
The president	16 (8.5%)	72 (38.1%)	61 (32.3%)	40 (21.2%)	2.34	.363	**.716**
Political issues	18 (9.5%)	56 (29.6%)	69 (36.5%)	46 (24.3%)	2.24	.349	**.762**
Congress	6 (3.2%)	19 (10.1%)	60 (31.7%)	104 (55.0%)	1.61	.180	**.901**
The Supreme Court	5 (2.6%)	13 (6.9%)	60 (31.6%)	111 (58.4%)	1.53	.172	**.863**

Note: Column figures are raw numbers of student respondents. Percentages appear in parentheses. Responses were indicated on a four-point Likert scale. All variables have been coded so *that higher values indicate a greater frequency of occurrence.* Factor solutions are varimax rotated.

indicates that there is a systematic difference between what students talk about with their parents, and what they talk about with their friends.

Perceptions About the Supreme Court and Its Members

Students were asked to say whether or not they felt that justices are politicians, and then to explain why or why not. This is important because justices benefit greatly by not being perceived as politicians; noncompliance is more likely to occur if the Court is viewed as merely another actor in the political process.

Table 6.4 shows how students perceived the justices. As noted above, most students indicated that Supreme Court justices are not politicians, primarily because "they aren't elected" or because "they just don't fit the definition of a politician." What is particularly striking is the contrast between how students in different classes answered the question. Students who had Mr. McGill were most likely to regard Supreme Court justices as politicians—over half of those students believed that they are. Only 16 per cent of students who had Mr. Caballero thought that justices are politicians. This is in the face of what appears to be a direct message to the contrary delivered by the teacher:

Junior high and high school kids are really into this idea of justice and "that's not fair" or "that's not right." If you can kind of open up a unit by bringing up one of those things: "OK, tell me what a democracy is all about." And then, "What if I told you that the people who basically decided that the schools be integrated that they're in it for life, unelected, powers can't be cut, that basically they have no accountability unless they commit an impeachable offense"—and that pumps them up a little bit. (Mr. Caballero).

So why do so few of his students see justices as politicians, and what accounts for the difference in perception between his students and those most willing to label justices as politicians (Mr. McGill's)? Recall that Mr. Caballero teaches in a parochial school, with what he considers to be "students of above average intelligence." Mr. McGill, on the other hand, is one of two American Government teachers at his school, and a substantial number of students in his class had failed the course the semester before and were taking it again to fulfill the requirement before graduation. What may be more interesting, however, is the difference in presentation and style between these two instructors.

Mr. McGill is cynical and dry-natured while Mr. Caballero is energetic and inquisitive, frustrated by tension between the constraints of his job and the endless possibilities of his students' interest. Environmental factors, however, interact with teaching philosophy and style. Mr. McGill gets away with showing Hollywood movies in his class, while Mr. Caballero is constantly reminded of the imposed parameters of discussion, as each class period begins with a prayer. He has a difficult time being critical or deviating from the curriculum (which, like the public schools, is system-friendly). He shows considerably more support for the political system than does Mr. McGill. It stands to reason

Table 6.4
Differences among American Government Teachers: Student Perceptions of
Supreme Court Justices

	Justices Are Politicians	Justices Are Not Politicians	Mean	N
Mr. Kaupas	15	23	.395	38
Mr. Caballero	7	38	.156	45
Mr. Hawk	11	21	.344	32
Mr. Peralta	11	24	.314	35
Mr. McGill	13	11	.542	24
TOTAL	57	117	.328	174

Note: All variables are dummy variables. A value of 1 indicates that the respondent felt that Supreme
   Court justices are politicians; a value of 0 indicates that he or she did not.

that the Catholic school students (or any other students) are less likely to think
Court justices are politicians than Mr. McGill's students are.

Do students in different classes similarly have different levels of diffuse support for the Court? Table 6.5 shows this clearly to be the case. Students in-
structed by Mr. McGill—those most likely to consider Supreme Court justices
to be politicians—are the least supportive of the Court, with a median right in
the center of the five-point scale. Most other classes are considerably more
supportive. To look at it another way, we might ask if there is a correlation
between a student's teacher and a student considering justices to be politicians
or having diffuse support for the Court. This is the case with some teachers'
students, but not with others (see Table 6.6). Again, Mr. Caballero and Mr.
McGill stand out, and the direction of the coefficients are consistent with what
we would expect: Mr. Caballero's students are less likely to consider the justices to be politicians and have a greater level of diffuse support for the Court,
while Mr. McGill's students are positively correlated with the likelihood of considering justices to be politicians, and have less support for the Court. All of
these correlations are moderate in magnitude. The other teachers, for the most
part, do not have a statistically significant effect on either of these two variables. That does not, of course, mean that there is no effect when other attitudes are controlled. Still, it is important to keep these differences in mind as
we construct a model to explain diffuse support for the Court among high
school students.

Table 6.5
Differences among American Government Teachers: Students' Diffuse Support for the Supreme Court

	Median	Mean	N
Mr. Kaupas	3.400	3.501	41
Mr. Caballero	3.800	3.956	45
Mr. Hawk	3.800	3.906	34
Mr. Peralta	3.800	3.672	39
Mr. McGill	3.000	3.077	26
TOTAL	3.600	3.664	185

Note: Teachers are dummy variables, while the diffuse support index is made up of the five survey items that loaded highly on the diffuse support factor reported in Table 6.1. Higher values on the index indicate greater levels of support.

Table 6.6
Correlation of Diffuse Support for the Court, Perception of Justices and American Government Teachers (Students)

	Are S.C. Justices Politicians?	*Diffuse Support Index*
Are S.C. Justices Politicians?	1.00	
Diffuse Support Index	-.301**	1.00
Mr. Kaupas	.076	-.125
Mr. Caballero	-.216**	.248**
Mr. Hawk	.016	.172*
Mr. Peralta	-.014	.006
Mr. McGill	.182*	-.356**

Note: Pearson's r correlation coefficients are reported. Teachers are dummy variables, while the diffuse support index is made up of the five survey items that loaded highly on the diffuse support factor reported in Table 6.1. Higher values on the index indicate greater levels of support and the belief that justices are politicians.

* $p < .05$; ** $p < .01$

Table 6.7
Correlation of Confidence in the Court, Congress, and the Federal Executive (Students)

	Confidence in Court	Confidence in Congress	Confidence in Executive	Diffuse Support Index (Court)
Confidence in Court	1.00			
Confidence in Congress	.398**	1.00		
Confidence in Executive	.317**	.460**	1.00	
Diffuse Support Index (Court)	.420**	.144	.068	1.00

Note: Pearson's *r* correlation coefficients are reported. Exact question wording appears in the Appendix. The diffuse support index is made up of the five survey items that loaded highly on the diffuse support factor reported in Table 6.1.

** p < .01

Other Variables Affecting Diffuse Support for the Court

As mentioned in chapter 3, previous research has found that the most important indicator of confidence in the Supreme Court has been confidence in the other two branches of government. Table 6.7 shows Pearson's *r* correlation coefficients for confidence in the people in all three branches of government, as well as the diffuse support index.[8]

The only variable that correlates significantly with the diffuse support index is confidence in the people running the Supreme Court. This is not surprising considering the aforementioned inability for most people to separate the institution of the Court from its members. Confidence in people running the two "political" branches of government correlates moderately with confidence in the people running the Court, suggesting that, like in the adult population, there is a general cynicism factor at work. In order to construct a model to begin to describe the root of diffuse support for the Court, we should first examine a series of bivariate and multivariate regression models, using the diffuse support index as the dependent variable.

There has been continued debate over the past few years as to the extent of the relationship between specific support for Court decisions and diffuse support for the Court. As evidenced by Table 6.1, these are two distinct factors, at least in the sample under consideration here. That does not mean, however, that diffuse support for the Court is not affected by specific support. Table 6.8 shows the results of several regressions on diffuse support for the Court. While the specific support for Court outputs indicator is statistically significant (model 1), the coefficient is small. This suggests that while specific support for the Court may have some effect on diffuse support, it is not particularly notable and certainly does not come close to explaining much of the variance in that index.

Similarly, the combined items measuring confidence in the people running Congress and the federal executive branch show statistical significance but do not appear to be as relevant in explaining diffuse support among this population as they are in the adult population, where, controlling for other factors, they are the most important predictors of support for the Court.[9]

Model 3 of Table 6.8 provides a further illustration of what was apparent in Table 6.5. This time, however, the effects of the other teachers are controlled as we examine the relationship between a student's diffuse support for the Supreme Court and his or her instructor. The constant in this model represents the mean of the students' responses from Mr. McGill's class, as that variable was randomly omitted for proper model specification. The coefficients can be interpreted as adding to the mean from that point. That is, we can recall that Mr. McGill's students had the lowest level of diffuse support for the Court. Thus, the coefficients for every other teacher are positive, indicating that we can add those figures to the mean of his students (represented by the constant) to predict how much more diffuse support exists among those teachers' students than the students who had Mr. McGill for American Government. This model alone, with no other considerations beyond the students' instructor, accounts for 17 per cent of the variance in the diffuse support scale. So far, this is the most important determinant of diffuse support for the Court.[10]

I stated above that the primary objective of this chapter was to show that political education does indeed matter with regard to high school students' support for the Supreme Court. Past models for adult attitudes have found the respondent's level of education (held constant in this study), confidence in the other two branches of government, and, to a lesser extent, support for Court decisions to be important indicators of diffuse support for the Court as an institution. Model 3 of Table 6.8 suggests that a student's teacher is also an important predictor for support (or lack of support) for the Court. Model 4 combines these findings to explain 23 per cent of the variance in support for the Court in this sample.[11] Keeping in mind that our dependent variable—diffuse support for the U.S. Supreme Court—is a five-item index measured on a five-point scale, we can interpret the constant as the level of diffuse support for respondents who have

- no agreement with any of the Court decisions about which they were asked (abortion, capital punishment, and mandatory prayer in public schools),
- no confidence at all in Congress or the federal executive, and
- Mr. McGill for American Government class.

Table 6.8
Predictors of Students' Diffuse Support for the Court: Comparison of Bivariate and Multivariate Models

	(1)	(2)	(3)	(4)
(constant)	2.442***	2.482***	2.077***	1.512***
Index of Specific Support for Court Outputs	.090 (.051)*			.139 (.051)**
Index of Confidence in Congress and the Federal Executive Branch		.176 (.095)*		.163 (.086)*
Mr. Kaupas			.430 (.152)**	.507 (.154)**
Mr. Caballero			.879 (.150)***	1.011 (.152)***
Mr. Hawk			.829 (.158)***	.809 (.154)***
Mr. Peralta			.595 (.154)***	.624 (.150)***
F	3.087*	3.432*	10.700***	9.753***
Adjusted R^2	.01	.013	.17	.23

Note: Coefficients reported are unstandardized. The dependent variable, diffuse support for the Court, is an index of the Caldeira and Gibson (1992) items, measured on a scale from 0 to 4. The dummy variable for students in Mr. McGill's class has been randomly omitted from the model for proper specification. Asterisks indicate statistical significance of corresponding t-values.

*** p < .001; ** p < .01; *p < .10

A student meeting those characteristics would score a 1.5 on the five-point diffuse support index, with zero being the least amount of support and four being the greatest amount. Since all of the predictor coefficients are positive, it can be said that the hypothetical student's score would increase by the coefficient for each unit he or she increases on the predictor scale. From this, we can see that, controlling for the other predictors in the model, having Mr. Caballero pushes a student's score up an entire point on the five-point index. A glance at the standaradized coefficients reveals that the teacher variables are the strongest predictors of support for the Court in this model. That suggests a more comprehensive examination of how differences among those teachers, the texts they choose, and/or the schools in which they teach, among other factors, influence the way students perceive the U.S. Supreme Court. We cannot estimate the strength of that relationship without considering what other factors also impact diffuse support for the Court.

Operationalization of Variables

Based on findings in the previous chapters and in the extant literature, we can expect certain variables to influence students' diffuse support for the Court. *Interpersonal communication* is an index of measures of media attentiveness and the student's frequency of interpersonal communication about politics with parents and peers.[12] *Media attentiveness* is composed of indicators of the frequency with which students watch local and network television news and read newspapers or news magazines, and a measure of general interest in politics.[13] If the hypothesis that more information tends to lead to a more critical view of politics holds, we should expect a negative coefficient for these two variables in the model.

Both *ideology* and *party identification* have been found to have some effect on support for the Court over the years.[14] The direction of the effect is dependent upon the current political administration and composition and activity of the Court. We should expect, then, that any effect would be in a positive direction, indicating that conservatives and Republicans, respectively, have more support for the Court. There should be little or no relationship here, however, since this population is less likely to have political structures and beliefs driving their attitudes. Further, these items have not had much explanatory power among the adult population in past studies either, and there is no reason to suspect more significant results among the high school students.

Since the U.S. Supreme Court is a relatively invisible institution, there is reason to believe that Americans' evaluation of it is contingent upon their overall perceptions of the justice system. Two indicators are included to test this hypothesis. I asked students about the so-called trial of the century, thinking that most of them would have followed it to some degree.[15] I asked if they believed that O. J. Simpson received a fair criminal trial and whether they believed that he killed Nicole Brown Simpson and Ronald Goldman. An affirmative response to the first question and a negative response to the second indicate that the student is *satisfied with the Simpson trial* (fair trial and a correct verdict).[16] Higher values of the variable (more satisfaction with the trial) should yield higher values in confidence in the Court, so we should expect the coefficient to be positive. Another measure of overall confidence in the judicial system is borrowed from Tom Tyler's (1990) study. I asked students the degree to which they agreed that "the American judicial system is the *best system* we could have."[17] Any effect should be in a positive direction.

Knowing more about the Court will only enhance respect for it if that information is overwhelmingly positive. For high school seniors whose primary source of knowledge about the Court is the schools, that information will, in fact, be positive. I asked students how many justices currently sit on the Court, and asked them to name as many as they could. *Knowledge about the Court* is an additive predictor combining two dummy variables: whether or not the student correctly indicated that there are nine justices on the Court, and whether or not the student could correctly name at least one justice. As noted above, this variable should produce a positive coefficient.

As evidenced in Table 6.6, students' support for the Court is correlated with their perception of Supreme Court justices. Specifically, if a student thinks of the justices as politicians, he or she will have less support for the institution. In the regression model, then, this dichotomous variable should have a negative coefficient.

Results

Table 6.9 shows seven different models designed to measure the effects of these predictors on support for the Court. Both interpersonal communication and media exposure are statistically significant in a positive direction. This is contrary to what was expected since the hypothesis is that the Court benefits by a *lack* of political information. If we reflect on this, however, it becomes apparent that the type of information the students are receiving from these sources is important.

In chapter 2, I argued that Congress and the president have higher negative ratings than the Court because of the difference in media coverage. Recall that the type of coverage is as important as the amount (a similar argument was made in chapter 5 regarding the textbooks). If the media is, as Davis (1994) notes, unlikely to cover the Court in a "personal" or "political" manner, increased media attentiveness or overall political communication should not adversely affect support for the Court. Indeed, models 1 and 2 of Table 6.9 are evidence of this.

As predicted, neither ideology nor partisanship has a statistically significant effect on support for the Court. Considering that even the adult population has generated mixed results with these predictors over the years, it is understandable that students with less developed ideological and partisan attachments would not use these factors to evaluate the Court.

Table 6.9
Predictors of Students' Diffuse Support for the Court: Interpersonal Communication, Media Exposure, and Other Political Attitudes

	(1)	(2)	(3)	(4)	(5)	(6)	(7)
(constant)	2.043***	2.067***	2.360***		2.778***	2.171***	1.881***
Interpersonal Communication	.307 (.075)***						.229 (.085)***
Media Exposure		.242 (.088)**					.016 (.095)
Ideology			.057 (.046)				
Party Identification			.040 (.033)				
Satisfied with OJ Simpson trial				-.172 (.177)			
American justice system is the best				.140 (.050)**			.090 (.048)
Knowledge of Court					.561 (.140)***		.381 (.140)**

Table 6.9 (continued)

	(1)	(2)	(3)	(4)	(5)	(6)	(7)
Justices politicians?						-.378 (.104)***	-.320 (.102)**
F	16.641***	7.512**	2.064	4.668*	15.925***	13.354***	8.853***
Adjusted R^2	.08	.04	.02	.04	.08	.06	.18

Note: Coefficients reported are unstandardized. The dependent variable, diffuse support for the Court, is an index of the Caldeira and Gibson (1992) items, measured on a scale from 0 to 4. Asterisks indicate statistical significance of corresponding t-values.

*** p < .001; ** p < .01; *p < .05

Satisfaction with the O. J. Simpson trial has no predictive power, but satisfaction with the American justice system does. A lack of variance in the Simpson indicator may explain its lack of statistical significance.[18] As expected, those students who believe that the American justice system is the best we can have tend to have more confidence in the Court than those students who do not.

Students who have more knowledge about the Court are more supportive of it. Again, it is necessary to reflect back on the way students learn about the Court. Since the Court is presented largely in the context of protecting and preserving civil rights and liberties, "knowledge" would naturally lead to support. Similarly, those students who think that Supreme Court justices are politicians are less supportive than those who are not.

Model 7 in Table 6.9 estimates the effect of all variables that significantly predicted support for the Court in the other six models. Interpersonal communication, knowledge about the Court, and perception of justices as politicians remain significant, while level of media exposure and the belief that the American justice system is the best are no longer notable once we control for the other factors.

Table 6.10 incorporates these variables, as well as those found to be important in Tables 6.8 and 6.9. What is immediately apparent is that the dummy variables for the individual teachers all remain strong indicators of support for the Court. The standardized coefficients (*beta*) indicate that they are the strongest predictors in the model. Specific support for Court decisions is also statistically significant but is not be particularly notable. The same might be said of knowledge about the Court and perception of Court justices; while still useful, controlling for the students' Government teacher moderates their explanatory power.[19] Confidence in the other branches of government—found to be the most important determinant of support for the Court in the adult samples that do not account for political education—is no longer significant once knowledge of the Court and perception of justices as politicians are controlled. Both of these variables are still significant, even after controlling for the students' teacher. To determine how much power the teacher variables have, we can compare the R^2 of Table 6.10 with a similar model, absent only the four teacher indicators. Doing so, we find that the model without the teachers has an R^2 of .18. A difference in F test reveals that the addition of the teacher variables is statistically significant at $p < .001$.[20] In short, the teachers are the most important predictor of student support for the Court.

Finally, I was curious about the effect to which the teachers' influence is moderated by the amount of interpersonal communication students have about politics. It might be that the teachers are particularly influential over those students who do not talk very much about politics with their friends and family (a large proportion of the sample) but not so influential over those who are learning about politics outside of the classroom. Table 6.11 presents a regression model identical to that in Table 6.10, but with interaction effects estimated for interpersonal communication and the students' teachers.[21] None of the interaction terms are significant, and the R^2 is not improved at all. Further, the teacher variables remain strong, which means that they are the best predictors, even controlling for the interaction effects.

Two of the four important determinants of a student's diffuse support for the Court related to political education are the student's teacher and how much the student knows about the Court. We also know that, at least with regard to some teachers (Mr. Caballero and Mr. McGill), perceptions of the justices are related to what teacher the student has for American Government (see Table 6.6). Clearly, political education must be considered when attempting to explain latent attitudes such as confidence in political institutions, particularly America's most invisible institution—the Supreme Court.

Table 6.10
Predictors of Students' Diffuse Support for the Court: Effects of Teachers and Other Explanatory Variables

	Coefficent (s.e.)	beta	t-value
(constant)	1.479 (.231)		6.394***
Index of Specific Support For Court Outputs	.118 (.050)	.170	2.357*
Index of Confidence in Congress and the Federal Executive Branch	.149 (.085)	.115	1.755
Interpersonal Communication	.111 (.079)	.104	1.405
Knowledge of Court	.320 (.135)	.160	2.368*
Justices Politicians?	-.196 (.097)	-.136	-2.016*
Mr. Kaupas	.432 (.152)	.263	2.842**
Mr. Caballero	.764 (.1687)	.491	4.544***
Mr. Hawk	.675 (.156)	.395	4.335***
Mr. Peralta	.503 (.149)	.310	3.375**
F	8.357***		
Adjusted R^2	.27		

Table 6.11
Predictors of Students' Diffuse Support for the Court: Interaction Effects of Teacher and Interpersonal Communication

	Coefficient (s.e.)	beta	t-value
(constant)	2.256 (.162)		13.944***
Index of Specific Support for Court Outputs	.116 (.050)	.166	2.314*
Index of Confidence in Congress and the Federal Executive Branch	.153 (.084)	.118	1.820
Interpersonal Communication (centered)	.135 (.079)	.126	1.704
Knowledge of Court	.332 (.136)	.166	2.451*
Justices Politicians?	-.182 (.097)	-.126	-1.884
Mr. Kaupas (centered)	.500 (.174)	.305	2.871**
Mr. Caballero (centered)	.932 (.189)	.599	4.923***
Mr. Hawk (centered)	.704 (.172)	.412	4.092***
Mr. Peralta (centered)	.599 (.178)	.369	3.372**
Mr. Kaupas (centered) X Interpersonal Communication	.342 (.292)	.121	1.171
Mr. Caballero (centered) X Interpersonal Communication	-.205 (.277)	-.089	-.740
Mr. Hawk (centered) X Interpersonal Communication	.149 (.305)	.048	.489
Mr. Peralta (centered) X Interpersonal Communication	.318 (.294)	.117	1.080
F	8.357***		
Adjusted R^2	.27		

NOTES

1. I feared that students who took the survey at home might consult their parents or others. A cross-tabulation of how many students were able to correctly name a currently sitting justice shows that students who took the survey home actually tied for the least likely to be able to name even one sitting justice. Similarly, those students were the least likely to be able to correctly indicate that nine justices sit on the Court (only 11 per cent were able to do so, compared to the total sample average of 30 per cent). Thus, there does not appear to be a bias favoring those students who completed the survey at home versus those who completed it in class.

2. The student sample is over 92 per cent white, while the adult sample is 83 per cent white.

3. Lower scores translate into more support for the Court in questions 1 through 4, while question 5 is worded in such a way that higher values indicate more support for the Court.

4. The index of diffuse support for the Court has a reliability measure (Kronbach's alpha) of .753.

5. It is worth noting that even the best students have similar attitudes toward the Court. I have spent one week each of the past few summers reading and evaluating the free-response portion of the Advance Placement examination in U.S. Government and Politics administered by the College Board and the Educational Testing Service. Students spend a semester or a year in an "advanced" Government course and, if successful on the AP exam, can receive college credit for the course. At the 1999 reading, I was reading a question that asked students to choose an interest group from a list of four and discuss what federal institution that group targeted and discuss two characteristics or resources the group uses to achieve its objectives. Students who chose the National Association for the Advancement of Colored People (NAACP) wisely noted that the group often targets the Supreme Court. Interestingly, the vast majority of these students argued that this was a good decision since the Court was above politics or did not make decisions based on the political beliefs of the justices.

6. Students were also asked about how often they listened to news on the radio, but there seemed to be some confusion about what that meant in terms of the difference between "news" on the radio and talk radio programs. Indeed, the news radio item loaded alone on a third factor during an exploratory principal components analysis and, for these reasons, has been dropped from consideration.

7. The two factors are correlated with one another at .686.

8. I was concerned that the question order might result in a contextual cue for the respondent. That is, if the specific support questions were asked first, respondents might be more likely to use specific support to determine answers to the diffuse support questions or vice-versa. During the pilot study, I used two forms (reversing the order of the specific and diffuse support items) and found no effects of cueing in either direction.

9. This is primarily because support for the Court in chapter 3 was measured by the question about confidence in the people running the Court, as the diffuse support index was not available for that sample.

10. Since the teacher variables are multi-category dummies, created from a nominal variable, it is necessary to conduct a difference in F test to determine if the increased power of the model with the variables is, in fact, due to their inclusion. This is done by comparing that model with a similar model, absent the teacher dummy variables. This test yields an F ratio of 11.93, which is statistically significant at $p < .001$ with 4 degrees of freedom in the numerator and 175 in the denominator.

11. All the predictors boast statistically significant t-values, and the signs of the coefficients are in the expected directions.

12. Kronbach's alpha = .897.

13. Kronbach's alpha = .595.

14. See Handberg and Maddox (1982); and Murphy and Tanenhaus (1968).

15. In fact, over half of the students reported following the Simpson criminal trial "very closely" or "somewhat closely."

16. These two variables correlate with a Pearson's r of .28 and are indexed to form a single predictor (Kronbach's alpha = .432).

17. Curiously, this variable does not correlate significantly with either of the questions about the O. J. Simpson trial. This does not mean, however, that it may not be a good predictor of support for the Court.

18. Only 8 per cent of the students were satisfied with the trial (variance = .073).

19. The model boasts an R^2 of .27 which is impressive compared to that of the model 7 in Table 6.9 (.18) and model 4 of Table 6.8 (.23).

20. The test yields an F ratio of 5.271 with 4 degrees of freedom in the numerator and 171 in the denominator. The critical F value for those degrees of freedom is 4.62 with a probability of .001.

21. Because of the multi-collinearity problem associated with interacting a multi-category dummy variable (teacher), it is necessary to center all terms in the interaction by subtracting the individual scores for each case by the mean of the variable. This was done for each of the four included teacher predictors, as well as for the interpersonal communication variable.

Chapter 7

Educating for Democracy: Lessons for Life

Americans are, by and large, increasingly dissatisfied with the public education system. According to the General Social Surveys data (Davis and Smith 1998), 49 per cent of Americans had "a great deal" of confidence in the people running the nation's educational institutions in 1974. By 1996, that number had dropped to around 23 per cent. Similarly, 18 per cent of Americans had "hardly any trust" at all in educators in 1996, compared to only 8 per cent who felt that way twenty years earlier. Beginning with *A Nation at Risk* (National Commission on Excellence in Education 1983), we have been barraged with reports and books that outline the failings of America's schools at all levels (see, for example, Bennett 1992, 1988, 1986, 1984; Bloom 1987; and Kozol 1991). While this study is certainly critical of the shortcomings of formal political education, there is reason to be optimistic.

Rather than a widespread, expensive overhaul of the educational system, a shift in priorities on the part of teachers and administrators will foster a commitment to a truly "critical" democratic education experience wherein students can learn the limits as well as the benefits of American democracy. This, in turn, will encourage them to evaluate (and embrace) their valuable position within the system.

A RENEWED FOCUS ON SOCIALIZATION

Simply asserting that a person's political education has an influence on the way he or she thinks about the Court while in school is interesting, but not particularly useful unless we can in some way relate it to attitudes in adulthood. Absent a panel study over a time, it is impossible to speak definitively about the persistence of political attitudes beyond adolescence. Still, it is useful to get a picture of what adolescents think and feel about the Court at the time they are learning most of what will be the basis of their education about American politics.

This book began with a discussion of judicial legitimacy. I noted that members of the U.S. Supreme Court necessarily rely on voluntary compliance to their rulings by lower courts, executive officials, and administrative agencies. While we are not all that much further toward explaining the root of the Court's support, an important finding occurred along the way: political learning may still be a quite important predictor for certain types of political attitudes. More important, we got a glimpse of what is really going on with our children's formal political education.

In 1991, Pamela Johnson Conover noted that "the subfield of political socialization is in trouble, serious trouble" (125). Scholars had turned their backs on an area of inquiry that, in the 1960s and 1970s, promised to answer some of the most elusive questions about political behavior and system stability. But these were promises never met. The "hippies" became living falsification of both the theories of hereditary political attitudes and the belief that children viewed politics in a "benevolent" manner—attitudes that were supposed to be solidified by adolescence. Further, there was increasing pressure from progressive political researchers who pointed out that work on the roots of political socialization tacitly promoted a conservative agenda since the socialization process is inherently system-reinforcing (Conover 1991). With the exception of those who continued to examine how socialization works on adults (for example, how attitudes change during higher education or after an employment change), political scientists abandoned trying to explain political behavior and attitudes by looking at early socialization or formal political education.

But the studies that served to dissuade socialization research were more interested in participation-related issues such as ideology, partisanship, and attitudes about salient political issues. I have argued that consistent with what we now understand about the continuing socialization process, political attitudes that go unchallenged throughout the course of one's adult life are more a product of one's early socialization or formal political education than are other, more salient, attitudes. This notion cuts against what has previously been assumed with regard to persistence.

The earlier literature suggests that while issue preferences are most likely to be volatile, more fundamental beliefs such as partisanship and ideology should persist into adulthood, thus making young children the most important subjects of research. But in this era of increased media attention to labels such as "conservative" and "liberal," these concepts are not as latent as they may have been in the past. In short, U.S. citizens may be thinking more in terms of partisanship and even ideology than they were thirty years ago.[1] If these concepts are increasingly in the public consciousness because their saliency has been heightened, their likelihood to change necessarily increases. On the other hand, citizens rarely talk about (or, I suspect, think about) their confidence or lack of confidence in various political institutions (especially the Supreme Court). These are some of the most latent (and, therefore, most stable) political attitudes. There is virtually no reason for the average citizen to ever consider his or her position with regard to system or institutional support. In fact, the only time that lack of thought is interrupted is most likely when a respondent is asked about his or her level of support for a public opinion survey. To answer accurately, it is necessary to reach back into one's memory and give an indication of that support. While these attitudes may very well be altered by a number of other factors (as we have seen in chapter 3), they are certainly the least volatile. They are, for the most part, developed during adolescent socialization (primarily through formal political education), and serve as the basis for diffuse support into adulthood.

REASONS FOR PERSISTENCE

Attitudes may go unchallenged for a number of reasons. Attitudes about the Court, we know, go unchallenged because there are far fewer stories about the Court in the mainstream media, and those stories that do exist tend to focus on the decisions made, not the justices personally or the decision-making process itself (Slotnick and Segal 1998; Davis 1994). But some political attitudes go unchallenged because they are simply so widely accepted that a challenge never arises. Tom Tyler (1990) provides a compelling study that suggests that people's attitudes toward the justice system are formed during the early socialization process and rest largely on normative assessments of right and wrong. We evaluate justice in our adult lives based on those conceptualizations of what is or is not just. In Tyler's study, it is the idea of "justice" that goes relatively unchallenged throughout one's life, so the normative values that were formed early on in childhood are likely to persist into adulthood. The lesson is that less salient political issues or institutions benefit from their relative invisibility. An institution such as the Supreme Court, which can operate meaningfully only with a sustained level of legitimacy, depends heavily on the support it develops early on in a young American's life and does not rely on popular agreement with individual decisions for its base of support.

It is inappropriate at this point to state definitively that formal political education is the most important indicator of how students will perceive the Court in adulthood. That link has not been empirically established. What the above findings do show, however, is that political education does matter in determining what adolescents think about the Court while they are in school.

We might rush to make a theoretical leap and claim that if this is the last substantial amount of information the student will receive about the Court, then there is reason to suspect persistence, but such a leap would be hasty at best. More work needs to be done to determine what it is about the teacher or the class (or even the school) that causes variations in levels of diffuse support for the Court. Further, we should attempt to empirically answer the question of persistence on this issue.

NORMATIVE IMPLICATIONS

I want to conclude with some suggestions for the direction that political education should take in this country in the twenty-first century. There is an interesting parallel between the role of Government teachers (who teach about, among other things, the courts) and the role of judges in the American legal system.

G. Alan Tarr (1994) distinguishes two types of judicial decision-making. The legal perspective expects judges and justices to "decide cases according to law, rather than on the basis of personal predilection or public opinion, and . . . justify their rulings through a process of legal reasoning." (268). This is the classic textbook definition of judicial decisionmaking. Another approach is the political perspective, where "extralegal factors, such as the attitudes of the judges, their conceptions of how they should behave, and the institutional context in which they operate" are most important (268-269). It is apparent that high school civics teachers have differing impacts on their students based on those same three factors: their attitudes, their conceptions of their duty, and the context of the school in which they teach.

Certainly we do not expect teachers to be as "objective" as we might wish judges to be, but there is a certain propensity to believe that our students are being similarly, if not equally, educated. That is the whole idea behind standards of civic education: "Content standards provide teachers with clear statements of what they should teach their students. They promote fairness by providing teachers with adequate notice of what is expected of them" (Center for Civic Education, 1994, 9). Reliance on textbooks for content and organization keeps teachers on virtually the same wavelength, but that is where the similarities end.

And what about that wavelength? In a review of American Civics and Government textbooks, James Carroll et al. (1987) hinted at the way these courses tend to treat students as "objects" rather than "subjects" in the political experience. They note that "[r]eaders are led to conclude that what is most important to learn about government is facts, facts, and more facts. Dates, names, and places abound, with little context to link them. What emerges is a portrait of government as lifeless institutions and mechanical processes, remote from politics and citizens" (i). These authors, writing for the civic-minded group People for the American Way, recognize that students need to see themselves as active participants in, not mere observers to, their political world.

Most educators would claim to be proponents of critical thinking, but the content of the material plays an important role in fostering a truly critical approach to educating for democracy. None of the teachers in the study introduced material that challenged the existing political structure of the U.S. government in my presence, nor did they claim in their interviews that they do so. If progressives are concerned about the system-reinforcing nature of American political (civic) education, this study will do nothing to alleviate their concerns. The only students who showed any resistance to the system were those of Mr. McGill, whose politics are less "progressive" or challenging to the system than they are cynical and, in some sense, disassociated. His attacks of politics in America were largely condescending to the students. I observed conversations where Mr. McGill would tell students something to the effect of: "If you think the government doesn't have a file on each of you, you're nuts." His interest seems to be genuine in that he wishes to point out to students that everything is not as it appears, but his failure to engage the class in any critical discussion about governmental structures or relations in no way fosters a climate of empowerment among his students.

Arguments that high school students are incapable of such discussions are unfounded. It is necessary, however, to have a dedicated facilitator for such dialogue. For example, I was in class for numerous discussions about political parties with at least two different teachers. Not once did a teacher offer that the two-party system is reinforced by a host of system-specific factors that make it extremely difficult for minor parties to win representation at any level of government. While a discussion of the differences between proportional representation and the single-member district plurality system can be difficult for students to understand, a little creativity can bring the topic to the level of students with much less education than high school seniors. Cutting an apple or a pie (or even a picture of a pie) would clearly demonstrate the way the United States' "winner take all" method of choosing representatives puts smaller party candidates at a disadvantage.

In place of such dialogue, the classes that I visited were consumed with the distribution of information in order to have that information recalled. That is not to say that teachers want students to learn only for the exam; I believe that all five teachers are sincere in their desire to help students become better informed citizens so that they can be active participants in the American political system. The problem is that all of these students' political activity will necessarily be confined within the parameters of the existing political structure. Paulo Freire (1968) argues that this type of atmosphere is not conducive to the kind of thinking that allows for liberation from an oppressive political mentality:

True dialogue cannot exist unless the dialoguers engage in critical thinking—thinking which discerns an indivisible solidarity between the world and men and admits of no dichotomy between them—thinking which perceives reality as process, as transformation, rather than as a static entity—thinking which does not separate itself from action, but constantly immerses itself in temporality without fear of the risks involved. Critical thinking contrasts with naïve thinking, which sees "historical time as a weight, a stratification of the acquisitions and experiences of the past," from which the present should emerge normalized and "well-behaved." For the naïve thinker, the important thing is accommodation to this normalized "today." For the critic, the important thing is the continuing transformation of reality, in behalf of the continuing humanization of men. (80-81)

The thinking that I witnessed during my time in these classes—on the part of both teacher and student—fits Freire's definition of "naïve." There is no sense that the students can be actors in any productive way other than that which is implied by the nature of the U.S. Constitution and the tradition of political participation (voting, contacting public officials, working on political campaigns, etc.). Students tacitly learn that any change must take place within the existing system ("accommodating this normalized 'today' "); changes to the system itself fall beyond the scope of U.S. citizens' formal political education. In this way, formal political education in the United States is, effectively, civic education.

If the goal of the schools, public or private, is to maintain support and legitimacy for the existing political structure in this country, then the drafters of those goals should take comfort in the revelation that U.S. schools are doing precisely that. If, however, we wish to move beyond the self-propagating masquerade of political learning in this country, it will be necessary to offer our children the type of education that allows them to come to an understanding not only of their political world, but of their important place within that world. Those are the most valuable lessons for life.

NOTE

1. In fact, the standard question wording from the American National Election Studies for the ideology item begins, "We hear a lot of talk these days about liberals and conservatives. . . . " This implies that when the question was designed, discussion in those terms was a relatively novel concept. That can hardly be considered the case today.

Appendix: Student Survey of Political Attitudes

On the following scale, please mark your level of partisanship:

☐Strong Democrat ☐Democrat ☐Independent Leaning Democrat

☐Independent ☐Independent Leaning Republican

☐Republican ☐Strong Republican ☐No Partisanship

☐Don't Know ☐Other_____

We hear a lot of talk these days about liberals and conservatives. Below is a seven-point scale on which the political views that people might hold are arranged from extremely liberal—point 1—to extremely conservative—point 7. Where would you place yourself on this scale?

☐1 extremely liberal ☐2 liberal ☐3 slightly liberal

☐4 moderate ☐5 slightly conservative ☐6 conservative

☐7 extremely conservative ☐Don't Know

For each of the following, please indicate how often you participate in the activity.

Read a daily newspaper

☐5-7 times per week   ☐2-4 times per week   ☐about once a week

☐never

Which one(s)?

_____

Read news magazines

☐5-7 times per week   ☐2-4 times per week   ☐about once a week

☐never

Which one(s)?

_____

Watch network news

☐5-7 times per week   ☐2-4 times per week   ☐about once a week

☐never

Watch local news

☐5-7 times per week   ☐2-4 times per week   ☐about once a week

☐never

Listen to news on radio

☐5-7 times per week   ☐2-4 times per week   ☐about once a week

☐never

Listen to talk radio

☐5-7 times per week   ☐2-4 times per week   ☐about once a week

☐never

When you do watch the news, do you usually watch it

☐alone   ☐with brothers or sisters   ☐with parent or parents

☐with entire family   ☐don't usually watch news

How often do you talk with your parents about:

political issues?
         ☐regularly   ☐sometimes   ☐hardly ever
         ☐never
Congress?
         ☐regularly   ☐sometimes   ☐hardly ever
         ☐never

the president?
         ☐regularly   ☐sometimes   ☐hardly ever
         ☐never

the Supreme Court?
         ☐regularly   ☐sometimes   ☐hardly ever
         ☐never

How often do you talk with your friends about:

political issues?
         ☐regularly   ☐sometimes   ☐hardly ever
         ☐never

Congress?
         ☐regularly   ☐sometimes   ☐hardly ever
         ☐never

the president?
         ☐regularly   ☐sometimes   ☐hardly ever
         ☐never

the Supreme Court?
         ☐regularly   ☐sometimes   ☐hardly ever
         ☐never

Some people seem to follow what's going on in government and public affairs most of the time, whether there's an election going on or not. Others aren't that interested. Would you say you follow what's going on in government and public affairs most of the time, some of the time, only now and then, or hardly at all?

☐most of the time   ☐some of the time   ☐only now and then

☐hardly at all

Please rank from 1 to 3 (1 being most interested) your interest in the activities of three branches of government.

_____Congress   _____President   _____Supreme Court

Below is a list of institutions in America. As far as the people running these institutions are concerned, would you say you have a great deal of confidence, only some confidence, or hardly any confidence in them at all?

The media
☐A great deal of confidence   ☐Only some confidence

☐Hardly any confidence

The military
☐A great deal of confidence   ☐Only some confidence

☐Hardly any confidence

Congress
☐A great deal of confidence   ☐Only some confidence

☐Hardly any confidence

The executive branch of the federal government
☐A great deal of confidence   ☐Only some confidence

☐Hardly any confidence

The U.S. Supreme Court
☐A great deal of confidence   ☐Only some confidence

☐Hardly any confidence

Major American political parties
☐A great deal of confidence   ☐Only some confidence

☐Hardly any confidence

Organized religion
☐A great deal of confidence   ☐Only some confidence

☐Hardly any confidence

What government agency or institution would you say best protects our rights and liberties?

_____

Please tell me whether you strongly agree, agree, disagree, or strongly disagree to the following statements:

> **"In a democracy, we all should be governed by the will of the majority, even if we disagree with it."**

☐Strongly Agree   ☐Agree   ☐Not Sure   ☐Disagree

☐Strongly Disagree

> **"A small group of people with a common interest should not be able to alter public policy for the entire country."**

☐Strongly Agree   ☐Agree   ☐Not Sure   ☐Disagree

☐Strongly Disagree

> **"People should obey the law even if it goes against what they think is right."**

☐Strongly Agree   ☐Agree   ☐Not Sure   ☐Disagree

☐Strongly Disagree

> **"Disobeying the law is seldom justified."**

☐Strongly Agree   ☐Agree   ☐Not Sure   ☐Disagree

☐Strongly Disagree

"Even though there are some problems, the American judicial system is the best system we could have."

☐Strongly Agree   ☐Agree   ☐Not Sure   ☐Disagree

☐Strongly Disagree

"The power of the Supreme Court to declare acts of Congress unconstitutional should be eliminated."

☐Strongly Agree   ☐Agree   ☐Not Sure   ☐Disagree

☐Strongly Disagree

"If the Supreme Court continually makes decisions that people disagree with, it might be better to do away with the Court altogether."

☐Strongly Agree   ☐Agree   ☐Not Sure   ☐Disagree

☐Strongly Disagree

"It would not make much difference to me if the United States Constitution were rewritten so as to reduce the powers of the Supreme Court."

☐Strongly Agree   ☐Agree   ☐Not Sure   ☐Disagree

☐Strongly Disagree

"The power of the Supreme Court to decide certain types of controversial issues should be limited by the Congress."

☐Strongly Agree   ☐Agree   ☐Not Sure   ☐Disagree

☐Strongly Disagree

"People should be willing to do everything they can to make sure that any proposal to abolish the Supreme Court is defeated."

☐Strongly Agree   ☐Agree   ☐Not Sure   ☐Disagree

☐Strongly Disagree

Do you think the Supreme Court is too liberal or too conservative or about right in its decisions?

☐Too Liberal   ☐Too Conservative   ☐About Right

☐Not Sure

> **"The United States Supreme Court was correct in ruling that a woman has the constitutional right to decide whether or not to carry a pregnancy to full term."**

☐Strongly Agree   ☐Agree   ☐Not Sure   ☐Disagree

☐Strongly Disagree

> **"The United States Supreme Court was correct in ruling that no state or local government may require the reading of the Lord's Prayer or Bible verses in public schools."**

☐Strongly Agree   ☐Agree   ☐Not Sure   ☐Disagree

☐Strongly Disagree

> **"The United States Supreme Court was correct in ruling that the death penalty for people convicted of murder is not, under most circumstances, cruel and unusual punishment."**

☐Strongly Agree   ☐Agree   ☐Not Sure   ☐Disagree

☐Strongly Disagree

What do you perceive to be the role of the Supreme Court?

Do you consider Supreme Court justices to be politicians?

☐yes   ☐no

Why or why not (a few sentences)?

How many justices currently sit on the U.S. Supreme Court? _____

Name as many justices currently sitting on the Court as you can.

How closely did you follow the O. J. Simpson criminal trial last year?
☐Very closely   ☐Somewhat closely   ☐Rarely

☐Not at all

Do you think O. J. Simpson received a fair criminal trial?
☐Yes   ☐No   ☐Not Sure

Do you think O.J. Simpson killed Nicole Brown Simpson and Ron Goldman?
☐Yes   ☐No   ☐Not Sure

What is your sex?

☐Male   ☐Female

What is your age?   _____

What are your plans after graduation?

_____

What race do you consider yourself to be?

☐White ☐Black   ☐Hispanic   ☐Asian/Pacific Islander   ☐other

Would you consider the area where you live urban, suburban, or rural?

☐Urban   ☐Suburban   ☐Rural

What   religion   do   you   consider   yourself   to be?_____

How much education do your parents have?

Father

☐More than four years of college   ☐Four years of college

☐High school degree or equivalent   ☐eight to twelve years of school
                                                                      (no degree)

☐Less than 8 years of school   ☐Don't know

Mother

☐More than four years of college   ☐Four years of college

☐High school degree or equivalent   ☐eight to twelve years of school
                                                                      (no degree)

☐Less than 8 years of school   ☐Don't know

References

Anderson, Christopher, Patricia G. Avery, Patricia V. Pederson, Elizabeth S. Smith, and John L. Sullivan. 1997. "Divergent Perspectives on Citizenship Education: A Q-Method Study and Survey of Social Studies Teachers." *American Educational Research Journal* 34:333-364.

Andrain, Charles F. 1971. *Children and Civic Awareness: A Study in Political Education.* Columbus, OH: Charles E. Merrill Publishing Company.

Apple, Michael W. 1993. *Official Knowledge: Democratic Education in a Conservative Age.* New York: Routledge.

Baum, Lawrence. 1976. "Implementation of Judicial Decisions: An Organizational Analysis." *American Politics Quarterly* 4:86-114.

Bennett, William J. 1992. *The De-valuing of America: The Fight for Our Culture and Our Children.* New York: Summit Books.

Bennett, William J. 1988. *Our Children and Our Country: Improving America's Schools and Affirming the Common Culture.* New York: Simon and Schuster.

Bennett, William. 1986. *First Lessons: A Report on Elementary Education in America.* Washington, DC: U.S. Department of Education.

Bennett, William. 1984. *To Reclaim a Legacy: Report on the Humanities in Higher Education.* Washington, DC: National Endowment for the Humanities.

Berkman, R., and L. W. Kitch. 1986. *Politics in the Media Age.* New York: McGraw-Hill.

Bloom, Allan. 1987. *The Closing of the American Mind: How Higher Education Has Failed Democracy and Impoverished the Souls of Today's Students.* New York: Simon and Schuster.

Caldeira, Gregory A. 1986. "Neither the Purse nor the Sword: Dynamics of Public Confidence in the Supreme Court." *American Political Science Review* 80:1209-1226.

Caldeira, Gregory A., and John L. Gibson. 1992. "The Etiology of Public Support for the Supreme Court." *American Journal of Political Science* 36:635-664.

124   References

Campbell, Angus, Philip E. Converse, Warren E. Miller, and Donald E. Stokes. [1960] 1980. *The American Voter* (unabridged edition). Chicago: The University of Chicago Press (Midway Reprint).

Carroll, James D., Walter D. Broadnax, Gloria Contreras, Thomas E. Mann, Norman J. Ornstein, and Judith Stiehm. 1987. *We the People: A Review of U.S. Government and Civics Textbooks*. Washington, DC: People for the American Way.

Casey, Gregory. 1976. "Popular Perceptions of Supreme Court Rulings." *American Politics Quarterly* 4:3-39.

Casper, Johnathan D. 1976. "The Supreme Court and National Policy Making." *American Political Science Review* 70:50-63.

Center for Civic Education. 1994. *National Standards for Civics and Government*. Calabasas, CA: Center for Civic Education.

Connell, R. W. 1971. *The Child's Construction of Politics*. Melbourne, Australia: Melbourne University Press.

Conover, Pamela Johnston. 1991. "Political Socialization: Where's the Politics?" In *Political Science: Looking to the Future* (vol. 3), ed. William J. Crotty. Evanston, IL: Northwestern University Press.

Dahl, Robert A. 1957. "Decision-Making in a Democracy: The Supreme Court as a National Policy-Maker." *Journal of Public Law* 6:279-295.

Davis, James Allan, and Tom W. Smith. 1998. *General Social Surveys, 1972-1998* (machine-readable data file). Chicago: National Opinion Research Center.

Davis, Richard. 1994. *Decisions and Images: The Supreme Court and the Press*. Englewood Cliffs, NJ: Prentice Hall.

Davis, Richard. 1992. *The Press and American Politics*. New York: Longman.

Dolbeare, Kenneth M., and Phillip E. Hammond. 1968. "The Political Party Basis of Attitudes Toward the Supreme Court." *Public Opinion Quarterly* 37:16-30.

Dometrius, N. C., and Sigelman, L. 1988. "Modeling the Impact of Supreme Court Decisions." *Journal of Politics* 50:131-149.

Dynneson, Thomas L., and Richard E. Gross. 1991. "The Educational Perspective: Citizenship Education in American Society." In *Social Science Perspectives on Citizenship Education*, eds. Richard E. Gross and Thomas L. Dynneson. New York: Teachers College Press.

Easton, David. 1965. *A Systems Analysis of Political Life*. New York: Wiley.

Easton, David, and J. Dennis. 1969. *Children in the Political System*. New York: McGraw-Hill.

Epstein, Lee, Jeffrey A. Segal, Harold J. Spaeth, and Thomas G. Walker. 1994. *The Supreme Court Compendium: Data, Decisions, and Developments*. Washington, DC: CQ Press.

Freire, Paulo. [1968] 1971. *Pedagogy of the Oppressed*. Translated by Myra Bergman Ramos. New York: Herder and Herder.

Gibson, John L., and Gregory A. Caldeira. 1992. "Blacks and the United States Supreme Court: Models of Diffuse Support." *The Journal of Politics* 54:1120-1145.

Giles, Michael W., Everett F. Cataldo, and Douglas S Gatlin. 1976. "White Flight and Percent Black: The Tipping Point Re-examined." *Social Science Quarterly* 56:85-92.

Graber, Doris A. 1997. *Mass Media and American Politics* (5th Ed.). Washington, DC: CQ Press.

Greenstein, Fred I. 1965. *Children and Politics*. New Haven: Yale University Press.

Greenstein, Fred I. 1960. "The Benevolent Leader: Children's Images of Political Authority." *American Political Science Review* 54:934-943.

Handberg, Roger. 1984. "Public Opinion and the United States Supreme Court, 1935-1981." *International Social Science Review* 59:3-13.

Handberg, Roger, and William S. Maddox. 1982. "Public Support for the Supreme Court in the 1970's." *American Politics Quarterly* 10:333-346.

Hansen, Susan B. 1980. "State Implementation of Supreme Court Decisions: Abortion Rates Since *Roe* v. *Wade.*" *Journal of Politics* 42:372-395.

Hardy, Richard J. 1996. *Government in America.* Evanston, IL: McDougal Littell/Houghton Mifflin.

Hibbing, John, and Elizabeth Theiss-Morse. 1995. *Congress as Public Enemy.* New York: Cambridge University Press.

Hirsch, E. D. 1993. *The Dictionary of Cultural Literacy.* Boston: Houghton Mifflin.

Hirsch, Herbert, and Lewis Donohew. 1968. "A Note on Negro-White Differences in Attitudes toward the Supreme Court." *Social Science Quarterly* 49:557-663.

Hyman, Herbert H. 1959. *Political Socialization: A Study in the Psychology of Political Behavior.* Glencoe, IL: The Free Press.

Ichilov, Orit. 1990. "Introduction." In *Political Socialization, Citizenship Education, and Democracy,* ed. Orit Ichilov. New York: Teachers College Press.

Jaros, Dean. 1973. *Socialization to Politics.* New York: Praeger.

Jennings, M. Kent, and Richard G. Niemi. 1981. *Generations and Politics: A Panel Study of Young Adults and Their Parents.* Princeton, NJ: Princeton University Press.

Jennings, M. Kent, and Richard G. Niemi. 1974. *The Political Character of Adolescence: The Influence of Families and Schools.* Princeton, NJ: Princeton University Press.

Johnson, Charles A. 1979. "Judicial Decisions and Organization Change: Some Theoretical and Empirical Notes on State Court Decisions and State Administrative Agencies." *Legal Studies Quarterly* 14:27-56.

Kozol, Jonathan. 1991. *Savage Inequalities.* New York: Crown.

Langton, Kenneth P., and M. Kent Jennings. [1968] 1973. "Political Socialization and the High School Civics Curriculum in the United States." In *Socialization to Politics,* ed. Jack Dennis. New York: John Wiley and Sons.

Lenart, Silvo. 1994. *Shaping Political Attitudes: The Impact of Interpersonal Communication and Mass Media.* Thousand Oaks, CA: Sage.

Manning, Peter K., and Betsy Cullum-Swan. 1994. "Narrative, Content, and Semiotic Analysis." In *Handbook of Qualitative Research,* ed. Norman K. Denzin and Yvonna S. Lincoln. Thousand Oaks, CA: Sage.

Marshall, Thomas R. 1989. *Public Opinion and the Supreme Court.* Boston: Unwin Hyman.

Marshall, Thomas R. 1987. "The Supreme Court as an Opinion Leader: Court Decisions and the Mass   Public." *American Politics Quarterly* 15:147-168.

Massialas, Byron G. 1972. "The School and the Political World of Children and Youth: An Overview." In *Political Youth, Traditional Schools: National and International Perspectives,* ed. Byron G. Massialas. Englewood Cliffs, NJ: Prentice Hall.

McClenaghan, William A. 1996. *Magruder's American Government.* Needham, MA: Prentice Hall.

Mishler, William, and Reginald S. Sheehan. 1993. "The Supreme Court as a Countermajoritarian Institution? The Impact of Public Opinion on Supreme Court Decisions." *American Political Science Review* 87:87-101.

Mondak, Jeffery, and Shannon Ishiyama Smithey. 1997. "The Dynamics of Public Support for the Supreme Court." *Journal of Politics* 59:1114-1142.

Moore, Stanley W., James Lare, and Kenneth Wagner. 1985. *The Child's Political World: A Longitudinal Perspective.* New York: Praeger.

Murphy, Walter F., and Joseph Tanenhaus. 1968. "Public Opinion and the United States Supreme Court: A Preliminary Mapping of Some Prerequisites for Court Legitimation of Regime Changes." *Law and Society Review* 2:357-382.

National Commission on Excellence in Education. 1983. *A Nation at Risk: The Imperative for Educational Reform : A Report to the Nation and the Secretary of Education, United States Department of Education.* Washington, DC: The Commission [Supt. of Docs., U.S. G.P.O. distributor].

O'Brien, David M. 1993. *Storm Center: The Supreme Court in American Politics* (3rd ed.). New York: W. W. Norton and Company.

Peters, C. Scott. 1995. "Public Support for the Supreme Court: Values, Awareness, and Contextual Information." Paper presented at the Midwest Political Science Association Meeting, Chicago, IL, April 6-8.

Plato. 1993. *Republic.* Translated by Robin Waterfield. New York: Oxford University Press.

Remy, Richard C. 1996. *United States Government: Democracy in Action.* New York: Glencoe.

Scarre, Geoffrey, ed. 1989. *Children, Parents and Politics.* New York: Cambridge University Press.

Secret, Phillip E., James B. Johnson, and Susan Welch. 1986. "Racial Differences in Attitudes Toward the Supreme Court's Decision on Prayer in Public Schools." *Social Science Quarterly* 67:877-885.

Segal, Jennifer. 1995. "Diffuse Support for the United States Supreme Court: Reliable Reservoir or Fickle Foundation?" Paper presented at the Midwest Political Science Association Meeting, Chicago, IL, April 6-8.

Sigel, Roberta S. 1989. *Political Learning in Adulthood: A Sourcebook of Theory and Research.* Chicago: The University of Chicago Press.

Sigelman, Lee. 1979. "Black and White Differences in Attitudes toward the Supreme Court: A Replication in the 1970's." *Social Science Quarterly* 60:113-119.

Slotnick, Elliot E., and Jennifer A. Segal. 1998. *Television News and the Supreme Court: All the News That's Fit to Air?* New York: Cambridge University Press.

Slotnick, Elliot, and Jennifer A. Segal. 1992. "Television News and the Supreme Court." Paper presented at the annual meeting of the American Political Science Association, Chicago, IL, September 3-6.

Sorauf, F. J. 1959. "*Zorach v. Clauson*: The Impact of a Supreme Court Decision." *American Political Science Review* 53:777-791.

Tanenhaus, Joseph, and Walter F. Murphy. 1981. "Patterns of Public Support for the Supreme Court: A Panel Study." *Journal of Politics* 43:24-39.

Tarr, G. Alan. 1994. *Judicial Process and Judicial Policymaking.* St. Paul, MN: West.

Turner, Mary Jane, Kenneth Switzer, and Charlotte Redden. 1996. *American Government: Principles and Practices.* New York: Glencoe.

Tyler, Tom R. 1990. *Why People Obey the Law.* New Haven, CT: Yale University Press.

Weber, Robert Phillip. 1990. *Basic Content Analysis* (2nd ed.). Newbury Park, CA: Sage.

West, Robin L. 1993. "Constitutional Scepticism." In *Contemporary Perspectives on Constitutional Interpretation*, ed. Susan J. Brison and Walter Sinnott-Armstrong. Boulder, CO: Westview.

CASES CITED

Abbington School District v. *Shempp.* 344 U.S. 203, 83 (1963)
Baker v. *Carr.* 369 U.S. 186, 82 (1962)
Brown v. *Topeka Board of Education.* 347 U.S. 483, 74 (1954)
Furman v. *Georgia.* 408 U.S. 238, 92 (1972)
Gregg v. *Georgia.* 428 U.S. 153, 96 (1976)
Lee v. *Weismann.* 505 U.S. 577 (1992)
Planned Parenthood of Southeastern Pennsylvania v. *Casey.* 505 U.S. 833 (1992)
Roe v. *Wade.* 410 U.S. 113, 93 (1973)
Wallace v. *Jaffree.* 472 U.S. 38, 105 (1985)
Webster v. *Reproductive Health Services.* 492 U.S. 490, 510 (1989)
Zorach v. *Clauson.* 343 U.S. 306, 72 (1952)

Index

About the Author

STEPHEN M. CALIENDO is a Visiting Assistant Professor of Political Science at the University of Missouri-St. Louis. His research focuses on public opinion, political communication, and political socialization. He has published in *The Harvard International Journal of Press/Politics* and the *Journal of Research in Science Teaching*.